CULTURE CHANGE

CHANGE

MADE EASY

CULTURE CHANGE MADE EASY

See Your Hidden Workplace Patterns and Get Unstuck

JAMIE NOTTER AND MADDIE GRANT

THINK TWICE
BOOKS

Washington, DC

Think Twice Books | www.thinktwicebooks.com

All trademarks are the property of their respective companies.

Cover Design: Matt Chase

Book Design: Zoe Norvell

Cataloging-in-Publication Data is on file with the Library of Congress.

ISBN: 978-1-64687-179-7

Special Sales

Think Twice books are available at a special discount for bulk purchases for sales promotions and premiums, or for use in corporate training programs. Special editions, including personalized covers, a custom foreword, corporate imprints, and bonus content, are also available.

To Catherine and Sarah,
our wonderful mothers, who taught us never
to stop asking the deeper questions.

Contents

Chapter 4: Heavy Agility — 91

Chapter 5: Incomplete Innovation — 119

Chapter 6: Getting Unstuck — 149

Chapter 7: Making the Change Happen — 177

Appendices — 193

CHAPTER 1

Culture Change Is in Your Hands

BOTTOM LINE

We all want exceptional workplace cultures that deliver better results and higher employee engagement. We know that companies with weak or average cultures struggle to attract and retain top talent.

But culture change seems daunting—it feels time-consuming, risky, and difficult to manage.

The real problem, however, is that we are not seeing the invisible patterns inside our culture that make culture change so hard. In this book we will show you those patterns and give you a model for changing your culture in ways that fix the problems created by the patterns—all in a matter of months, not years.

When you learn how to accelerate your culture change, you will achieve new levels of success you didn't think were possible. Whoever changes culture the fastest wins, which is exactly why we want to make culture change easier.

To equip you for this journey, this initial chapter defines key terms like "culture," "Culture Patterns," and "culture change" and gives you concrete advice on how to get started with your culture change, no matter where you sit in your organization. It also maps out the rest of the content in the book for you.

We also put additional resources for you online at culturechangemade easybook.com.

So how did we crack the code on culture change? We (Jamie Notter and Maddie Grant, the book's co-authors) have spent the last 20+ years working with organizations of all sizes as management consultants, but with a twist—something unique that makes our work different. Jamie's background is in conflict resolution, generations, and organization development, and Maddie's is in digital strategy and online communities. Added together, that means our lens continuously focuses on integrating the human aspects of work with the digital.

The digital age brought tremendous change to the workplace, now accelerating exponentially as artificial intelligence (AI) gets thrown into the mix. The business world must adapt to this continuous digital revolution in ways that enable the humans who work in our organizations to thrive.

The good news is that we're sitting on 1.2 million data points about workplace culture that we have collected over the last 8 years, and they have given us the key to how to do just that. That key is the Culture Patterns we are about to show you.

Buckle up.

Busting the Myths About Culture

But first… a word of caution.

Several years ago, we watched a panel of CEOs discussing workplace culture at a small conference. One was the prominent CEO of a well-respected company, and when it was their turn to present, they made an announcement that we thought was quite provocative:

"It takes a minimum of eight years to change a culture."

We expected to hear murmurs or pushback from the crowd. We've been in the culture field for a long time and have seen plenty of cultures change significantly in less than eight years. The most extreme example we saw was a nonprofit in Arizona with about 300 employees that did a complete culture turnaround in only twelve months. They went from an oppressive culture of fear, where senior managers only came down to the main floor out of their upper-level executive offices when they needed to yell at or fire someone, to a vibrant, healthy culture of empowered and engaged employees—in only about a year. That kind of transformation takes hard work (and likely a high number of "employee separations" during that year), but the idea that culture change takes a minimum of eight years struck us as ludicrous.

Yet the audience responded to the CEO's assertion with nods of approval, jotting down these words of wisdom on their conference notepads. The message resonated with them because, for a very long time, conventional wisdom has been telling us that culture and culture change are hard to get your hands around. Who hasn't heard that "workplace culture is a vibe," a sense, an atmosphere, created by everyone in the organization? It's just "the way we do things here," so it's nebulous. It's how your employees feel about working there, so it's internal to them, thus tough to change.

As leaders, conventional wisdom argues, we cannot control or direct culture, so changing it requires us to coax and cajole our employees to embrace the new culture we are promoting, which rarely works. According to *Harvard Business Review*, a company with 1,000 employees spends, on average, $2.2 million annually trying to improve culture. Yet, only 30% of Chief

Human Resource Officers feel they're getting a good return on that investment.[1] Conventional wisdom is clear: culture change is hard.

As the saying goes, however, conventional wisdom is often neither conventional nor wise. In this case, it's flat-out wrong. Let's start by busting a few culture myths here.

MYTH: Culture is hard to define.
REALITY: Culture is easy to understand and measure.

Culture is the collection of words, actions, thoughts, and tangible aspects of work that clarify and reinforce what is truly valued inside an organization. We break this definition down for you later on in this chapter, and while there is some complexity to it (for example, sometimes the behaviors inside your culture end up contradicting the words you use to describe it), the truth is, it's not hard to understand or measure.

MYTH: Culture is hard to change.
REALITY: You've been changing your culture all along and probably didn't realize it.

If you change internal processes (like your meetings or your budgeting process), design new structures (like your org chart or your office design), or change how you use technology (like your communications channels or your customer database), you will produce a visibly different culture in months, weeks, or even days. In fact, if you ignore culture entirely, yet make significant changes in those three areas (process, structure, technology), then your culture will change without you even noticing. There is no doubt that culture change takes effort—everything worth doing does—but it is no more challenging than the other problems that you effectively solve on a regular basis.

And, as we will show you in this book, **culture change becomes much easier when you see your Culture Patterns.** The existence of Culture Patterns

1 The Wrong Ways to Strengthen Culture." Harvard Business Review, July 2019. https://hbr.org/2019/07/the-wrong-ways-to-strengthen-culture. Accessed September 2023.

is the biggest lesson we have learned from our research and practice in the eight years since we created our culture assessment. Culture Patterns make visible the competing commitments inside your culture that create an insidious drag on performance. Seeing your Culture Patterns changes the game. Those internal contradictions can then become the focus of the changes you make to your processes, structures, and technologies, and the result is a more effective culture that makes your people more successful.

Most of this book is devoted to revealing and understanding the Culture Patterns we identified in our research. **Chapters 2 through 5 cover the four primary Culture Patterns related to collaboration, transparency, agility, and innovation.** We will present the competing commitments inside each Culture Pattern, including their negative impacts on performance. For each one, we will provide a case study or examples of organizations that have found a way to transform the pattern in their culture and generate impressive results.

MYTH: Culture and culture change must come from the top.
REALITY: Everyone reading this book can change their culture.

Once we started tackling culture change by addressing the Culture Patterns, we learned the most powerful lesson: senior leaders *do* play a critical role in designing and sustaining an effective culture, but that doesn't change the fact that culture change is in the hands of everyone inside the organization.

Culture change must happen at every level of the hierarchy and in every functional area to be effective. This means it can start within a single department or team, just as much as it can start with the management team deciding what Culture Patterns they want to transform. Culture change is systemic, so we designed the model for culture change that we offer in this book to be leveraged by every part of the system. No one part of the system can transform culture by itself, but similarly, every single part of the system can start to change the culture on its own.

Chapter 6 lays out a simple but effective culture change model that you can use immediately. We use a "playbook" metaphor, and there are six different categories of plays for changing culture. We mentioned the first three categories above: process, structure/design, and technology. The next three categories focus more on sustaining your culture and culture change efforts: talent and human resources, rituals and artifacts, and culture stewardship. Chapter 6 covers all this, and **the final chapter offers advice for doing culture change top-down and bottom-up at the same time.**

Conventional wisdom is wrong about culture, and because we've been following its advice for decades, most of us are in organizations with weak cultures that are holding us back from reaching our potential. We wrote this book because we want to turn that around.

Core Concepts of Culture and Culture Change

Before we get into the nitty-gritty of how to change culture in chapters 2-6, let's get on the same page on the core concepts, specifically:

- What is culture?
- What are Culture Patterns?
- What is culture change?
- How do you start?

What Is Culture?

We have been writing about culture for more than a decade, and we've developed a concise definition. Back in 2011, when we wrote our first book, *Humanize: How People-Centric Organizations Succeed in a Social World*, we succumbed a little to conventional wisdom ourselves, claiming that single-sentence definitions of culture weren't useful and didn't help you improve things.[2] We then went on to write four paragraphs explaining

---

2 Jamie Notter and Maddie Grant, *Humanize: How People-Centric Organizations Succeed in a Social World* (Indianapolis, IN: Que Publishing, 2012), p. 66.

what culture is in terms of "walk," "talk," and "thought." Just two years later, we wrote our first e-book on culture, and by then, we had broken free from the grips of conventional wisdom and came up with the first draft of what we now use as a clear definition of culture:

> Culture is the collection of words, actions, thoughts, and "stuff" (tangible aspects of work) that clarifies and reinforces what is truly valued inside an organization.

Culture is ultimately about what is *valued* because what is valued drives behavior. That's why they say "culture eats strategy for breakfast." Strategy is a conceptualization of behaviors that will drive an organization's success, but if what is deeply valued in your culture is driving very different behaviors, then your strategy is unlikely to succeed, no matter how brilliant it is.

But culture isn't just about the values. It exists in the collection of words, actions, thoughts, and stuff inside your organization. That's where we see it, understand it, and change it, so let's break that down.

Words

Human beings make sense of the world through story, so language is critical, and that's why we start with the words we use to define our workplace cultures. A big part of our culture is what we say it is, because it is through our words that we create a shared understanding of culture. So, to do culture right, you must be very clear and disciplined with the words you use to describe your culture, both internally and externally.

Unfortunately, most organizations do a horrible job at this. Imagine conducting a job interview with a candidate that you desperately want to hire. When you ask the candidate if they have any questions for you, you are likely to get, "So, what is the culture like here?"

Take a minute now and write down your answer in two or three paragraphs. It doesn't have to be perfect, but jot down the key ideas, points, or concepts you would use to describe your culture. Frequently, when we ask leaders to do this, we see a lot that falls into the following categories:

- **Vague.** They describe their culture using terms like "good," "strong," or "healthy." Or they talk about how much the staff likes the culture (without actually describing it). These descriptions are not objectionable, but the candidate still has no clear understanding of what it would be like to work there.
- **Over-simplified.** The most common response is to rattle off the organizational core values. Unfortunately, the true meaning of values like collaboration, customer focus, or accountability, for example, is difficult to discern in only one or two words. In addition, there are too many examples of companies that tout core values but don't live them (e.g., Enron, Wells Fargo, etc.), so unless you provide detail, it's hard for the candidate to believe even these simple words.
- **Metaphorical.** Or they use high-level metaphors to describe the culture, like saying that the company is like a "family" or a "well-oiled machine." The problem here is that what you mean by family may differ greatly from what the candidate means by family. For those of you who use the family metaphor, remember that the number one word in the English language associated with the word family is "dysfunctional!"

Instead, you should be clear and detailed in explaining what is valued in your culture and why. If you have a core value of collaboration, you should answer the question with something like this:

> "Well, collaboration is one of our core values, and we really are quite obsessed with it. Everyone here works on multiple cross-functional teams, and now that we're in the office only a few days a week, we got rid of the private offices and replaced them with communal tables where people can easily start conversations with their colleagues. This constant communication enables us to spot issues and problems earlier on, so we stay a step ahead of our customers, and they love that. If you're the kind of person who just wants to put on their headphones and plug away on your individual work, you won't like it here."

That description provides behavioral details that back up the core value and clarifies why they have built that culture (e.g., because customers love it). Note, however, that having a collaborative culture is not the point here. This response would be equally effective:

> "Well, one thing that surprises people is that we are rigidly siloed here, and that's on purpose. Everyone stays in their swim lanes, so to speak. Teams remain laser-focused on their deliverables and don't want to be distracted by getting involved in other teams' activities. Given our product and market, this approach gives us incredible speed, and that's how we beat our competition, so if you're the kind of person who thrives on cross-functional teams and open office floor plans, you won't like it here."

That describes a very different culture, but it still meets the requirement of an effective description: (1) it paints a tangible picture of what it's like to work there, and (2) it connects the culture with what makes the organization successful. If you describe what your culture values but don't explain *why* those aspects are valued, your answer is much more difficult for candidates to trust. It sounds like lip service or what you think they want to hear. **Culture is not about sounding good or appearing cool. It should be about being good in ways that make the organization (and the candidate who is imagining working there) more successful.**

Actions

Once you find the most effective language to describe your culture, you should then focus on the actions, or behaviors inside your culture. As the saying goes, actions speak louder than words, so you should pay attention to consistency. If the behaviors inside your culture are inconsistent with the language you used to describe it, the behaviors will end up defining the culture.

Let's say you told the candidate in the job interview that you had a culture of empowerment, hiring smart people and then letting them run with things; micromanaging is discouraged. Then, a few weeks into their tenure, the newly hired employee is walking down the hall, and their manager stops them to ask about a project they had been discussing the week before.

The new employee explains that the project is finished and is already live on the website, which takes the manager a bit by surprise, and they ask "Did anybody get to review that before it went live?" That single behavior by the manager just contradicted those words you used to describe the culture of empowerment. The new employee now realizes that it is not a culture of empowerment—it's a culture of approval hoops.

And that may be just fine. There's nothing wrong with reviewing and approving things; it may not harm that employee's engagement. The point is that the behaviors differed from the words, and the behaviors always win.

While that example may be innocuous, this component of culture management does have some real dangers associated with it. In their book *School Culture Rewired*, Steve Gruenert and Todd Whitaker coined a phrase about culture that the business world has widely adopted: "The culture of any organization is created by the worst behavior the leader is willing to tolerate."

The classic example is the senior manager who is a stellar producer with deep expertise but who treats people badly along the way. The organization feels they cannot afford to lose this person because of their performance or knowledge, so they tolerate their bad behavior, writing it off as an exception to the culture. But it doesn't work that way. Everyone sees the bad behavior, which becomes a very real part of the culture.

This example highlights something else about behaviors as a driver of culture: senior-level behaviors matter more. Everyone tends to look "up" when evaluating the consistency of words and actions in a culture. If my peer behaves in a way inconsistent with the culture, I might let it slide, figuring that person was having a bad day. But if a senior leader does the same thing, I'm frustrated because it proves that the culture is not what they've been saying it is.

That might strike you as unfair, but that is the responsibility of being a leader. You will be held to a higher standard regarding your behaviors if you want to maintain a strong culture. Leadership teams should have regular and frank conversations about where their behavior might be sending the wrong signals about the culture.

Thoughts

Most of the cultural inconsistencies you will be dealing with are behavior-based, but sometimes, you need to dig deeper and get into the realm of thoughts. Thoughts, in a cultural context, refer to deeper beliefs, assumptions, mental models, and worldviews of employees that drive behaviors that contradict the espoused culture. These thoughts are often not conscious or explicit, making them difficult to spot.

We once worked with a management team that claimed to have created a results-only work environment (ROWE). ROWE was made popular by Jodi Thompson and Cali Ressler, who experimented with the approach at Best Buy in the early 2000s. The approach is rooted in autonomy and clear metrics. Instead of forcing employees to work specific hours every weekday, give them crystal-clear metrics on the results they should be achieving, and then let them make their own decisions about how they achieve those results, including when—and where—they do their work.

When the management team took a break during our meeting, something interesting happened. Two of the senior managers started to gripe about the behaviors of some of their employees, specifically that one of them was consistently arriving to work at 10:00 a.m. and that another had left the office at 3:00 p.m. without telling anyone where they were going.

When we reconvened the leadership team, we confirmed with the group that in a results-oriented work environment, it doesn't matter when people come to work or leave work as long as they achieve their results—and they all agreed! They couldn't see the contradiction between their behavior (griping about when people come and leave) and the culture they thought they were creating (ROWE), and that's because most of them subscribed to a deeper belief that they didn't realize was getting in the way:

If I can't see you, you're not working.

As we learned during the pandemic, there is not a lot of logic behind this belief, but that doesn't stop people from subscribing to it. In a ROWE culture, rooted specifically in letting employees decide when and where they do their work, the belief can generate behaviors that weaken the culture. Those two managers were likely putting subtle pressure on employees to spend more time in the office, like praising those who spent less time working remotely. So sometimes, you need to make sure these deeper beliefs are consistent with what you want your culture to be.

Stuff

The last area of cultural consistency you must manage is in the tangible aspects of work (the "stuff"). The first three components are the human part of the culture—humans speak, act, and think—but all workplaces also have non-human aspects as well, including the office's design and location, the equipment used, and even the dress code. These tangible aspects of work can clarify and reinforce what is valued in the organization, so they are a part of what defines the culture.

In our 2015 book *When Millennials Take Over: Preparing for the Ridiculously Optimistic Future of Business*, we profiled the American Society for Surgery of the Hand (ASSH) as a case study. One aspect we did not share in that case study, however, was ASSH's dress code at the time, which was included in their printed policy manual, even though it was only two words:

No nudity.

If you show up to work at ASSH and are not naked, then you're good to go. Beyond that, you can wear anything you want. When we were at the office doing our research for the book, the CEO pulled aside an employee wearing shorts, sandals, and a Chicago Blackhawks jersey and proudly announced that this was their Director of Finance.

The CEO was proud of this because he strongly believes that authenticity drives improved performance. If his people can be their whole selves, he finds they are more engaged at work and produce better results.

So, the way he worded his dress code is not random or an attempt to be cute. He realized that if he wanted a culture based on radical authenticity, it would be inconsistent to have a tangible aspect of work—dress code—that says you can only wear jeans on Friday. As with words, actions, and thoughts, the goal here is to maintain consistency regarding tangible aspects of work and the culture you are trying to create.

What is Valued

Remember, everything we just discussed—words, actions, thoughts, and stuff—is there to clarify and reinforce what is truly valued in your organization, because what is valued will drive behaviors. This can be different, by the way, from what an organization espouses as core values. Just ask Enron, who literally had "honesty" and "integrity" hanging on the wall of their lobby, yet their entire management team went to jail for fraud. At Enron, the collection of words, actions, thoughts, and stuff must have implied that honesty was not valued as much as making your numbers—even if you have to make a large accounting firm lie about it. We never did research at Enron, so we don't know what was in place to make it clear to their employees what was valued, but it must have been there, because that is the behavior they got, regardless of what was posted on the wall.

On a more positive note, there are examples of organizations whose core values align tightly with what is valued (and, therefore, behavior). One of the more famous examples is Zappos. Their number one core value was to "WOW the customer with service," but they didn't just put that on a poster on the wall. They designed the organization carefully to generate that amazing customer service behavior.

In their onboarding process, for example, they sent every new employee through two weeks of customer service training, and then had them work another two weeks as a customer service representative answering customer calls. Every single hire went through this process, so even if you were a high-powered corporate attorney going to work for Zappos back then, you'd spend two weeks in training and then two weeks on the phones.

Years ago, we delivered a webinar where we told the story of this part of the Zappos culture, and we joked about how disappointing it might be if we ended up getting the lawyer when we called Zappos for service. At the end of the webinar, during the question-and-answer portion, someone in the audience explained that they worked for Zappos, and we had nothing to worry about... "We only hire lawyers who are good at customer service."

Most organizations fall somewhere in between Enron and Zappos. They will have a clear understanding of what is valued, but when they look internally, they see that the behaviors are not 100% aligned with what's valued. It may not be the exact opposite (as it was at Enron), but the alignment is off. An organization might be serious in its commitment to internal collaboration, for example, yet it suffers from the frustrating effect of silos and internal competition. It could value transparency and information sharing, yet people there are frustrated because information is often shared too little too late. This dynamic is extremely common and rooted in a concept at the very heart of this book: Culture Patterns.

What Are Culture Patterns?

A Culture Pattern exists when what is valued by your culture is not being lived fully or as intended, as in the case of collaboration and transparency mentioned above. It is not that collaboration or transparency are completely absent. On the contrary, they happen all the time, just not at the level leaders really want or at the level that drives the success of the organization.

If that tension or contradiction feels familiar to you, it should, because you are human. As humans, we all have values, but most of us do not live those values consistently or fully. One of the key reasons for that is something that researchers Robert Kegan and Lisa Laskow Lahey refer to as "competing commitments."

As they explain in their book, *Immunity to Change,* we all have commitments, goals, or things we want to achieve, yet when we take a look at our own behaviors, we often discover that we are doing things that specifically work against our own commitments.[3] Why is that?

It is because there is a hidden, competing commitment that is driving our ineffective behaviors. You may be committed to doing a good job at work, for example, but you are also committed to being a good spouse, parent, and friend, and if you push your work commitment too hard at work, you will likely engage in behaviors that make it harder to meet your commitments to family, friends, and your health.

The age-old "work-life balance" conundrum is an obvious example of a personal competing commitment. This came into focus when the 2020 pandemic hit, and home life and work life suddenly were sharing the same physical space. A lot of people began to re-evaluate the importance of home and family and started rethinking, reprioritizing, and rebalancing (or really, reintegrating) their work commitments with their personal commitments and priorities. Hence the Great Resignation and its long-lasting effects on the business world, which are still continuing to take place (a subject for another book in the future, perhaps).

Some competing commitments are harder to spot. Maybe your commitment to quality family time spent over long dinners competes with your commitment to losing weight. Maybe your commitment to finding some downtime to relax your brain in front of the TV competes with your commitment to getting healthier through exercise. Resistance to change is not simply opposition to something—it's driven by another commitment, something that is important to you, even though you may not realize it. Seeing that commitment and figuring out how to reconcile it with your original commitment is critical for change to be successful.

We bring this up because **competing commitments are at the heart of your hidden Culture Patterns.** In the workplace, you have many competing commitments. Your commitment to achieving your departmental goals may actually compete with your commitment to collaborating with other

---

3 Robert Kegan and Lisa Laskow Lahey, *Immunity to Change: How to Overcome it and Unlock the Potential in Yourself and Your Organization* (Cambridge, MA: Harvard Business Press, 2009).

teams. Your commitment to building relationships across the organization through organic water cooler conversations competes with your commitment to finishing your to-do list. In fact, even though you're reading this book about culture change, your commitment to changing culture could be in competition with your commitment to cross things off your lengthy to-do list! But don't despair. Research shows that competing commitments can be resolved, but you have to see them clearly first.

In the context of workplace culture, **our data shows that if you dig under the surface, you can frequently find a competing commitment that neutralizes key elements of what your culture values.** We mentioned above that many organizations are committed to collaboration, for example, but it turns out they also have a commitment to giving autonomy to individual departments. This makes collaboration more difficult: departments, units, or layers in the hierarchy inside the organization insist on their own autonomy, which makes getting groups of people to collaborate across those lines more difficult. Cross-group collaboration happens, but not without extra effort and often frustration.

That is a Culture Pattern. The competing commitment (e.g. between collaboration and subgroup autonomy) results in being unable to live the value of collaboration fully or as intended. Both commitments are valid, but the way they square off against each other in the culture ends up neutralizing the cultural value of collaboration.

We call that pattern in particular "Awkward Collaboration," where a culture values collaborative individuals more than it values collaborative groups, and we'll dig into it fully in Chapter 2. We identified the pattern by studying the aggregate data from the culture assessment that we created in 2016 (we now have nearly 20,000 completed surveys). It was one of eight primary Culture Patterns that live inside the eight culture markers that we measure in the WorkXO culture assessment:
- **Agility** - how an employer removes obstacles, distributes control and responsibility, uses processes and systems, manages change, and speeds into action
- **Collaboration** - how an employer facilitates exchange

and interaction, sets up teams to accomplish goals, shares knowledge and credit, and leverages relationships

- **Growth** - how an employer teaches, develops, rewards, champions health and welfare, facilitates the pursuit of passion, gives back, and acts as steward to the community
- **Inclusion** - how an employer orchestrates diversity and promotes authenticity, fosters respect and support, facilitates open participation and belonging, and creates a sense of ownership
- **Innovation** - how an employer encourages and rewards experimentation, provides challenging work, takes risks, fuels creativity, is comfortable with mistakes, and is compelled by what might be next
- **Solutions** - how an employer pays attention to unique internal and external user needs, anticipates and adapts to shifting landscapes/ markets, and creates solutions for clients and employees
- **Technologies** - how an employer invests in, leverages, and exploits current technology, next generation tools and business practices; leverages the digital age, and adopts new technologies
- **Transparency** - how an employer builds trust, demonstrates integrity, shares information openly, communicates clearly and truthfully, and is comfortable with emotion

These are not uncommon concepts in culture assessments, but the WorkXO assessment differs from others in that it does not establish favorable or unfavorable scores in these eight areas (the classic green, yellow, red continuum). Instead, **scores are presented along a continuum representing traditional to contemporary to futurist.**

This structure was critical in revealing the Culture Patterns, so here's what we mean by those terms.

Traditional means aligned with traditional management, which refers to management practices that embrace the command-and-control approach that was established and perfected during the 20th century, following the Industrial Revolution. Workplace cultures (or elements of those cultures) that score in our model as traditional tend to favor concepts like privacy, exclusivity, risk aversion, predictability, slow-and-steady, measured change with heavy change management, and an emphasis on the corporation rather than the individual.

Contemporary refers to cultures and organizations that have worked to evolve their management practices to move beyond the traditional practices of the 20th century but have not quite pushed the envelope far enough to be aligned with what we are now seeing as the "future of work." They have started to embrace ideas that are gaining popular acceptance these days in areas like experimentation, sharing information across silo lines, investing in professional development for employees, keeping updated on recent technology, valuing diversity, promoting internal collaboration, and focusing on customer service. But they still haven't strayed too far from the roots of traditional management, so the advances they make in areas like transparency, agility, or innovation are limited.

Futurist is a label we use for cultures that are consistent with organizations that have transformed their management practices in ways that are setting the standards for where we are headed in the future of work. In short, they are more human-centric. They favor concepts like a rigorous focus on users both internally and externally, constant innovation and improvement, extensive transparency to enable better decision-making, fluid and flexible hierarchies, and systems of trust that unleash surprising speed and agility. The case studies from our book *When Millennials Take Over*, are good examples of futurist cultures, but we've seen others in the business literature and our consulting work as well.

To be clear, **not everyone needs to be futurist in everything.** That's not the point. A nuclear power plant should not be super futurist on innovation—taking risks, hacking things and running lots of experiments—but a software company may realize that a futurist approach like that may be the only way they will beat the competition. Every organization will need to make its own call on how futurist it needs to be. In the aggregate data, the overall average score is 3.69 on a five-point Likert scale. Above 4 is futurist and below 3 is traditional, so, on average, we're moving toward futurist, but we're not quite there yet.

That, of course, is the key point here. We're trying to be more futurist, but we're not fully doing it. That sounds like a competing commitment is at play, doesn't it? We accidentally discovered the prevalence of the eight primary Culture Patterns by choosing the traditional to futurist continuum. **Within each of the key areas of culture we analyze, there are competing commitments that create a Culture Pattern that is preventing most of us from getting where we need to be.**

The Eight Primary Culture Patterns

These competing commitments generate a consistent pattern within each of the eight elements of culture that we measure. Some aspects of each culture marker were consistently more present in the culture (i.e., more futurist) than other aspects, and the parts that were more traditional were driven by a competing commitment.

We made reference above to the competing commitment inside collaboration—where we value helping each other out in the culture, but the competing commitment to the autonomy of subgroups makes the collaboration more difficult or awkward. This generates a consistent pattern in the assessment data, where the parts of the culture about how *individuals* collaborate with each other score more futurist, but the parts about how *groups* work together score more traditional. In other words, we value collaborative individuals more than collaborative groups, which is the Culture Pattern we started to see over and over again.

Each of the 8 Culture Patterns reveals an imbalance with what's valued inside the culture:

(see page 20)

CULTURE PATTERN	VALUE IMBALANCE
Awkward Collaboration	Valuing collaborative individuals more than collaborative groups.
Lagging Transparency	Valuing reactive transparency more than proactive transparency.
Heavy Agility	Valuing forward action more than effective action.
Incomplete Innovation	Valuing the concepts of innovation more than the practices of innovation.
Intangible Growth	Valuing aspirational growth more than developmental growth.
Shallow Solutions	Valuing solving problems more than meeting needs.
Micro Inclusion	Valuing personal inclusion more than structural inclusion.
Incrementally Digital	Valuing digital concepts more than digital tools.

In chapters 2 through 5, we're going to break down the top four patterns around collaboration, transparency, agility, and innovation, because they seem the most widespread. When organizations choose to improve their culture, they often focus on these areas over the other four. In Appendix A you will find a brief description of all 8 Culture Patterns.

Why Culture Patterns Matter

Culture patterns don't just exist—they cause problems. To use a fluid dynamics metaphor, Culture Patterns produce drag. The shape of a racing sailboat's hull is designed specifically to minimize the amount of drag created as it moves through the water, thus maximizing speed. But if something alters the shape of that hull—like, for instance, barnacles that attach to it—then drag is increased, and the boat will not go as fast as it could.

Culture patterns and the competing commitments inside them do the same thing in organizations: they create drag, resulting in missed opportunities, frustrated efforts, unsatisfactory or minimal C-grade results, and stagnation. Drag creates resistance to change, and it can be overt, but it can also be insidiously hidden in the organization's fabric.

In the next four chapters, we will break down the nuances of each Culture Pattern and how it shows up inside organizations, and then give you concrete advice on how to fix the resulting problems.

Once you see the Culture Patterns hidden inside your workplace culture, you can immediately start to fix them without too much effort, thereby creating positive culture change—without a huge organization-wide culture initiative and without necessarily having buy-in from everyone in your organization. This is what makes culture change "easy."

Of course, that presumes we're all on the same page about what culture change is.

What Is Culture Change?

That's the million-dollar question. We understand what culture is—words, actions, thoughts, and stuff that clarify and reinforce what is valued—and we now realize there are underlying Culture Patterns, based on competing commitments, that are creating drag and messing with our success. So how do we fix it?.

We know conventional wisdom tells you culture change is hard, but here's a simple definition:

Culture change is achieved by intentionally changing processes, structures, and/or technologies in order to drive new behaviors that make your organization more successful and enable the full expression of what is valued.

Let's give you a simple example. Imagine you are leading an organization that has the Culture Pattern of Awkward Collaboration, so your culture values collaborative individuals more than it values collaborative groups. That means you probably suffer from the ubiquitous "silo" problem. Departments and functions operate a little too independently, so you end up missing opportunities for growth, and areas like customer service suffer due to the lack of coordination and integrated effort across departments.

All you need to do to change your culture, per our definition above, is figure out what processes, structures, or technologies you could change in order to drive behaviors that would enable more effective collaboration among groups. Creating some cross-functional teams to tackle specific problems would be a simple structural change that you could implement right away. Or you could introduce some new processes, like a monthly meeting of middle managers from all departments to work through shared challenges. Or you could change how groups use technology, like your project management software. Instead of letting each department choose their own (thereby making their work invisible to the other departments), get everyone trained and active on one software solution for the whole organization (we'll talk about how one organization did just that in the case study in Chapter 2 on Awkward Collaboration).

Those three changes to structure, process, and technology may not transform your Awkward Collaboration pattern overnight, but they will start the process. If you combine those changes with others, and also add work on nurturing and sustaining your new culture over time, then your culture change will become both real and permanent. But you need to be systematic about it, and to do that we recommend you create a playbook.

The Culture Playbook Model

In Chapter 6, we will go over the Playbook Model for culture change in a lot more detail, but here's the bottom line. There are six different categories of "culture plays" that you can run to change and manage your culture, including the three we just mentioned, process, structure, and technology.

- **Process.** Your organization is a big bundle of operational processes, so changing them (as in the middle managers meeting example above) is where most of your culture change will come from.
- **Structure and design.** This category includes organizational structure (org chart, cross-functional teams) and physical structure (office space).
- **Technology.** The software you use to get work done can greatly impact specific elements of your culture, so this is a powerful lever.
- **Human resources and talent.** When you're changing your culture, by definition you'll need to change things like performance reviews and onboarding, so HR/talent/people management gets its own category of plays.
- **Rituals and artifacts.** Events and objects that communicate what your culture is to internal and external audiences.
- **Stewardship.** Intentional efforts to manage and sustain your culture over time.

Culture change happens when you design and run plays in these six areas. You'll want a good mix of plays, including quick wins and big ideas, and the right balance of plays that either fix culture issues or sustain and protect the elements of culture that make your business special.

Feel free to skip ahead to Chapter 6 if you want to read more about the Culture Playbook model before continuing.

How Do You Start?

One of the most important elements of this culture change model is that it is available to everyone, no matter where you sit in your organization. This book is a resource for you, so here's how to use it.

The next four chapters will show you how four major Culture Patterns operate, and you can use that to diagnose your own organization. **Read the first section of each chapter ("Bottom Line"). Do you recognize that Culture Pattern or its effects on your business? If you don't, then skip that chapter.** You can read it later, or never. We won't be offended.

If you do recognize it, read through for a longer explanation of how it shows up in the data, as well as a case study of what it looks like in a real-world company. You'll see how that particular organization solved for that Culture Pattern using specific interventions we call culture plays. But those examples are not the only culture plays that exist. At the end of the chapter we'll provide a short list of other plays we've come across that have worked. This list is purposefully short—it works better when you come up with your own.

Once you recognize a Culture Pattern existing in your own organization, it should become VERY EASY to come up with a bunch of ideas for how to fix it. We include some questions to ask yourself about your own business to prompt some brainstorming, and if you need more ideas, head over to culturechangemadeeasybook.com to browse for more. (And hey, if you have already solved for this particular Culture Pattern, please submit your culture plays to benefit others!). We also created some companion resources there. Go check them out when you have a moment.

Work through each of the Culture Patterns in the same way.

1. Identify where the Culture Pattern exists in your organization.
2. Brainstorm some ways to address it (culture plays).
3. Put them into action and change your culture.

Badabing badaboom!

…We know what you're thinking: it can't be that easy.

We promise you it is… but of course, not every idea and intervention will have the same level of effort. Chapter 6 covers a deeper dive into the playbook model for culture change that you can use to design your own culture change activities. You'll want to find the low-hanging fruit—the quick wins, the things you have control over, the things everybody already hates—before you can tackle the really big ones.

How do you eat an elephant? One bite at a time.

This book gives you the bites. (Metaphorically speaking only, of course. We love elephants and would never eat any.)

So jump in, because the organizations that change culture the fastest in today's rapidly changing environment will retain the best talent and beat the competition. The time to start is now.

CHAPTER 2

Awkward Collaboration

BOTTOM LINE

Organizations that suffer from Awkward Collaboration value collaborative individuals more than they value collaborative groups.

- We excel at creating cultures where people are generally willing to help each other. They know how to connect with each other and facilitate their collaborative efforts to be effective.
- We struggle, however, when groups inside the organization need to collaborate. Departments and functions have not figured out how to collaborate effectively, and the decision-making hierarchy, while important, ends up creating divisions within collaborative activities that make success more elusive.
- These organizations have a commitment to collaboration that is neutralized by a commitment to the autonomy of subgroups. They care about collaboration, but when it happens it tends to be awkward and less effective than it could be.

The problem with this Culture Pattern is that it creates collaborative gaps.
- Due to lack of trust, incomplete information, and unclear roles, collaborative activities have gaps that make them less effective and take longer.
- These gaps are hard to spot because the collaboration is somewhat successful, but opportunities are missed and potential is lost.

The solution to this problem is to reduce cognitive load and make the hierarchy more accessible.
- Our case study organization changed its culture by investing in decision-making role clarity and a comprehensive project management system that clarified what was happening and why, in ways that made collaboration more effective, particularly across functions.
- They also developed a mindset and specific processes that enabled the top of the hierarchy and the bottom of the hierarchy to work together more in partnership, which increased speed and engagement.

How You Can Solve It:
- **See your Culture Pattern:** identify the areas where this pattern is messing with success (we call this "culture friction"), like departments competing for control or the senior level getting too involved in projects.
- **Get unstuck:** run culture plays like shadowing programs or training in conflict resolution or facilitation.

Can Collaboration Be a Bad Thing?

Several years ago, we facilitated a senior management team retreat where the company was specifically focused on improving collaboration at the senior level. At one critical moment in the conversation, there was some back and forth about how important collaboration should be, and one of the Vice Presidents finally stopped holding back what she had been wanting to say for some time:

> "Do you want to know how I define collaboration? I define it as interference!"

The rest of the group was taken aback a bit, but once she explained her position, it had some logic to it. This particular leader was in charge of a division of the organization that accounted for 70% of its annual revenue. Several of the other VPs, in fact, wouldn't be able to run their divisions successfully unless the VP in question was successful in bringing in all that revenue.

So, her argument was simple: to collaborate more at the senior level, she would need to divert her attention away from that key revenue-generation function. In that way, collaboration would be interfering with her ability to deliver on that critical revenue promise. So, it wasn't that she thought working together was a bad thing; she simply didn't want to let the rest of the team down by letting collaboration interfere with her revenue delivery.

The truth is collaboration takes work. It takes communication, coordination, teaching, learning, listening, exploring, testing, and compromise. We have all had those moments when we're faced with an opportunity to collaborate on something with a colleague but end up just doing it ourselves because it is easier and faster to do so.

So why do we collaborate? Because the investment in the extra effort that collaboration requires usually provides a good return. It's called synergy, and we explored this in our first book, *Humanize*:

> "Collaboration (at the risk of turning our readers off with a buzzword) must achieve synergy. It's not enough to provide valuable help to a colleague in another department

to solve that particular problem. That's a good start, but we also need to be building that colleague's capacity along the way (or the capacity of others in the system) so that at the end of the project, *the whole system is able to solve future problems more easily. That is generative collaboration.* We need that kind of collaboration to get out of the mess we've created with today's organizations.[1]

That kind of generative collaboration is what that management team was trying to get at. There was no denying that there was some speed and efficiency to be achieved if everyone simply stayed in their swim lanes, but they could also see the downside: missed opportunities. Like any organization, they had many moving parts connected in many different ways, and opportunities to extract more value from that complex system can only be achieved through collaboration.

This organization had multiple revenue streams from the same customer base, but what if the different product lines weren't collaborating effectively? They would probably deliver communications or customer events that didn't take advantage of cross-selling opportunities. Or what if customer service rarely collaborated with product development? They would probably be missing opportunities to add features that customer service knew customers wanted, which would impact sales. In short, they'd be leaving money on the table.

This management team was so focused on that 70% of revenue number that they were missing the opportunity for growth. Collaboration may be a distraction, but it's worth it if it can boost overall revenue, even if that one department's revenue drops. Generating 50% of $12 million is better for everyone than 70% of $10 million. Once she saw the potential, that VP became a consistent champion for increased collaboration at the leadership team level.

That organization, unfortunately, is not typical. While every organization on the planet thinks collaboration is a good thing, most are leaving

---

1 Notter and Grant, *Humanize* (2012), p. 200.

a lot of money on the table and failing to achieve the synergy we mentioned above. The reason lies in one of the four primary Culture Patterns: Awkward Collaboration.

The Problem: Awkward Collaboration

Does any of this sound familiar?
- You've got good collaboration among individuals within teams, but when you try to collaborate across different teams, it misfires or takes too long.
- Your shared services departments (marketing, IT) are constantly fighting with your other programs, so those programs make their own mini versions of the functions internally.
- If you ask for help from someone in another department, they usually say yes but often fail to deliver on time.
- As soon as more than one layer in your hierarchy gets involved in a project, you can count on it going over budget and falling behind schedule.
- Conversations about "who's in charge" take up more of your time than "who's doing it."

These are classic examples of the Awkward Collaboration pattern. **Collaboration is happening, but organizations are falling short of their potential. Collaboration takes too long, produces less than optimal results, and generates employee frustration.** Why? Because organizations don't realize that they are placing a different value on how groups collaborate compared to how individuals collaborate, which is at the heart of this pattern.

What is Awkward Collaboration?

Organizations with the Awkward Collaboration Culture Pattern value collaborative individuals more than they value collaborative groups.

In other words, they're creating cultures where people are very willing to help each other out, but it's mostly person-to-person, and they are not emphasizing how whole departments or different levels of the hierarchy should be collaborating more effectively.

Like all Culture Patterns, it is rooted in a competing commitment. In this case, the commitment to working together is clear and strong, but it is neutralized by an equally strong commitment to the autonomy of subgroups. There is nothing inherently wrong with departments or levels in the hierarchy having appropriate levels of autonomy and independence. After all, why would you create departments if they aren't in charge of their area? However, if the competing commitment is not managed, collaboration across groups becomes ineffective.

Collaboration is a visible part of the culture in these organizations, but it is uncoordinated or awkward. There is every intention of collaborating with others, but the involvement of other departments is done inconsistently or after it's too late. Similarly, coordination across layers in the hierarchy lacks consistency or, worse, is intentionally overlooked. Whether collaboration is defined as essential or as interference is a moving target—it depends on who you ask and in what context.

We saw this pattern emerge in the aggregate data from our culture assessment. Over and over again, questions relating to how individuals collaborate, like "sharing the workload," "facilitation," and "relationship building," were showing up as very present inside the cultures, but the questions that focused on collaborative groups (including our measures of "borders, boundaries, and territories" and "cross-functional communication") were not experienced as much. This pattern can cause significant problems inside organizations.

How Awkward Collaboration Shows Up: Collaborative Gaps

The damage that Awkward Collaboration does inside organizations is sometimes difficult to spot, because most organizations value collaboration and can consistently point to collaborative activities that appear successful.

They put on an event, for example, and the participants were generally happy. They implement a new software system, and employees are able to use it. But if you have Awkward Collaboration in your culture, you are probably falling short of your potential.

Consider the event planning example. Your event planning staff is in charge of identifying all the content providers for the event, and the standard is high. Most of your participants come back year after year, so if the staff were to start serving up the "usual suspects" as content leaders every year, you risk boring the participants and seeing a decline in attendance.

But your event planners are not subject matter experts in the content that your participants are coming to see—that expertise exists in your programmatic departments. So, naturally, the event staff will reach out to the program staff for some help in identifying the best speakers.

Here's where Awkward Collaboration kicks in. Over the years, the program staff have come to resent the event staff for what they see as an over-reliance on their expertise. From their perspective, they are incredibly busy doing their own jobs, and then every year, at a certain time, the event staff start asking them to find speakers—which sounds an awful lot like an event planning task. They think to themselves, "why are you making us do your job?"

So this year, when the request comes in, the program staff reluctantly agree to help (again), but they end up dragging their feet. It's not intentional sabotage—they truly are busy, and they find it hard to prioritize this additional task given to them, so it slips. As the deadline approaches, the event staff start getting nervous and hounding the program staff for updates on the progress. This only serves to remind the program staff of how annoyed they were to begin with, so it does not spur them into action. Faced with the unpleasant result of having an open spot in the program, the event staff are forced to pivot, and they find an alternative speaker outside of that program's area of expertise.

Ultimately, the event happens, and the participants, as mentioned above, are generally satisfied. However, the collaborative gap did have an impact. Instead of getting cutting-edge programmatic expertise in that speaking slot, they ended up with one of the usual subjects or a topic that was slightly less relevant. The participants notice, even if it doesn't appear specifically in the evaluations. If this collaborative gap persists, the event could suffer a "death by 1,000 cuts," as content quality slowly declines (along with registrations).

It's not only horizontal silos that create collaborative gaps, however. The vertical hierarchy can be equally guilty. Large digital change projects are especially prone to this type of gap. Let's say your organization has hit the point where it has to upgrade a big internal database system. We all know that kind of change is hard and disruptive, but when your organization has outgrown the previous system, you basically have no choice.

The success of the change initiative will rely heavily on how well your middle management collaborates with other levels in the hierarchy. There are a lot of moving parts in this project, and there are a lot of decisions that need to be made quickly to effectively sequence and coordinate all the activities. Unfortunately, your middle management layer wants too much control over the process, so they have been leaving the senior level out of the loop, for fear that they will step in and overly influence how the work gets done.

That approach ultimately backfires, however, because by the time the senior level is brought in to give the green light on several key deliverables, they feel blindsided. They should have had visibility into the progress and direction of the project over the last month, but because they were not informed of key decisions and actions, they now feel uncomfortable giving the green light on the next phase without knowing more about the current status.

That then requires a repeat of several project status meetings to bring them up to speed, and with their busy schedules, it takes an additional month to complete the update meetings. This throws the whole project behind schedule, and in the future phases, the same thing happens.

In the end, the software gets implemented, and people start using it, but not without the business having wasted tremendous amounts of time—not to mention huge cost overruns for the consultants who had to spend more time than anticipated supporting the project. We often write off these delays and expenses as "the way it is" with complex technology change projects, but much of it could have been avoided without the hierarchical collaborative gaps that exist.

As you can see, Awkward Collaboration creates costly collaborative gaps. If you want to eliminate the gaps, then you need to understand the inner workings of how this pattern operates.

Breaking the Pattern Down: Collaborative Individuals v. Collaborative Groups

Like all of the Culture Patterns we describe in this book, Awkward Collaboration is rooted in a competing commitment. **In this case, the commitment to working together well is neutralized by the commitment to the autonomy of subgroups.** As a result, organizations end up with one part of collaboration where they excel, and one part where they struggle. We excel at valuing collaborative individuals, but we struggle when it comes to valuing collaborative groups.

In this section, we will dig into the data from our research a little bit. We have almost 20,000 completed surveys from our culture assessment, and the data paint some clear pictures of these patterns. As a reminder, all of the Culture Markers and Building Blocks we will be describing below are measured on a five-point scale, where a score below 3 is considered traditional, between 3 and 4 is contemporary, and above 4 is futurist (and if numbers bore you, just skim over those parts!).

Where We Excel: Collaborative Individuals

In traditional management, collaboration was de-emphasized. Management back then was based on how machines work, so yes, the various cogs in the machine did need to work together in concert, but that collaboration was designed at the top. It was enforced rather than spontaneous. The cogs didn't need to look for opportunities to collaborate or go out of their way to help others—they performed their prescribed role, and the collaboration happened automatically.

Today, most organizations have abandoned that approach. In our aggregate culture assessment data, Collaboration scores 3.80 out of 5, second only to inclusion among the 8 Culture Markers that we measure. Though if you look a little closer at the data, you'll notice that there are three specific Building Blocks that are driving that high average score:

- Sharing the workload
- Facilitation
- Relationship building

Those three combined average 4.12, qualifying as futurist in our scale. When you ask people in organizations if their co-workers are willing to help out when asked, almost everyone says yes, that's true most or all the time here (sharing the workload). The same is true when it comes to people being good facilitators and intentionally building relationships to help get the work done. Where traditional management essentially forced collaboration to happen, the cultures of today expect individuals to spontaneously help each other out, work together well, and intentionally make the collaboration process as easy as possible.

If your culture values collaborative individuals, you should have lots of examples of "above and beyond" collaboration. Not just simple examples, like "last week I asked my colleague to draft some copy for our email campaign and they did." They are more like that time your deadline got moved up by a week, and you pulled in a few extra people who stopped what they were doing and spent nearly a whole day helping you to finish the deliverable on time. The individuals in your organization don't collaborate grudgingly, they are enthusiastic about it.

You'll have numerous stories where things got heated as the deadline pressure mounted, but your people stepped up and skillfully facilitated a problem-solving session that got you out of a jam. Remember, the root of the word "facilitation" is facile, so it's about making things easy. For cultures that embrace facilitation, even the departments that are known for having rigid processes that sometimes drive people crazy (looking at you, accounting and IT) will be known for bending when necessary to make things easier for employees. **People are always on the lookout for ways to make things easier for their colleagues, rather than being head down, and focused on their own work.**

And you'll be intentional about relationship building in your culture, which has taken on a few new wrinkles now that remote and hybrid work are much more widespread. Many have complained that it has become harder to maintain good working relationships now that people are in the office less frequently.. While that has been a challenge, there are solutions out there. **Organizations that are good at relationship building will find ways to do it, even when everyone is not in the office.** We developed this chart to clarify some of the nuances involved in this new hybrid work environment:

THE NEW LOOK OF COLLABORATION

	INTENTIONAL	ORGANIC	
RELATIONSHIP FOCUSED	team-building retreat	chat in kitchen hallway conversation	*in-person*
	virtual happy hour	asynchronous channels	*virtual*
TASK FOCUSED	meetings	stop by an office hallway conversation	*in-person*
	video meetings	chat/IM	*virtual*

There are both task-focused collaborative activities and relationship-focused ones. The task-focused ones get more of our attention because that's what collaboration naturally looks like: people coming together to get something done. But you'll never maximize the value of collaboration if you aren't intentionally building and developing relationships, and organizations do that all the time through activities like staff retreats, happy hours, and casual interactions in the office.

In addition, there is a distinction between collaborative activities that are intentional versus ones that are organic. This distinction became very noticeable when we all went remote back in 2020. We realized that we had been relying on casual interactions in the office that were unplanned, and that's harder to do on Zoom or Teams. These "random hallway conversations" turned out to be very important, both for building relationships and solving real work problems.

But there ARE ways to do that virtually, which is why we divided all four boxes in the two-by-two matrix above to include both in-person and virtual components. You shouldn't do ALL of your relationship-building virtually if you are a hybrid workplace, but it doesn't require everyone to be back at the office all the time either. You'll need to strike a balance.

However you manage collaboration in the hybrid workplace, though, remember that **most organizations are still too focused on collaboration on an individual basis and don't pay enough attention to how groups collaborate.**

Where We Struggle: Collaborative Groups

While most organizations have deviated from traditional management by creating cultures that truly value collaborative individuals who help each other out, facilitate, and build relationships, they have not been as successful at letting go of one of the anchors of traditional management: the division of labor.

One of the main reasons we were able to scale our economies in the industrial era was by mastering the division of labor. Whether it was clear hierarchies or functional silos, ensuring that the right people were doing the right work was critical to success in traditional organizations. It allowed for much greater efficiency, since different components of the work could be carved out for the people with specific expertise to complete the tasks. Coordination of complex tasks was simpler, and cost control and quality were easier to maintain over a complex operation.

Division of labor, of course, is not going away. Even in the post-industrial world, it makes sense that marketing experts will gather together in a department where they can apply their deep expertise to solve the marketing problems that would confound those of us who lack that expertise. Similarly, if everyone in the organization has the exact same level of decision-making authority, then efficiency and strategic effectiveness become nearly impossible, so hierarchies also make sense. **As much as we say we hate them, silos and hierarchies are important. They reduce complexity and allow for more effective decisions and action.**

But they clearly have their downsides. As we wrote in our 2015 book *When Millennials Take Over*, the real problem with hierarchies is how rigid they are:

> Management hierarchies were invented in a simpler time. Railroad tracks don't move. You could design a decision-making structure for managing track work at a single point in time and safely expect it to work the same way for years to come, because the tracks don't change. We scaled operations of many types of organizations very quickly using this approach, so it has always been a given that organizations could design a complete decision-making authority structure and expect it to work as it was designed every time, in every context.... But in the internet age, nothing is static. We all recognize that the pace of change has gone through the roof and that disruption is the norm now, so why are we relying on static, inflexible, and thus vertical hierarchies?[2]

The truth is, as useful as hierarchies and departments can be in theory, most organizations have not learned how to make the most of them in practice. As the definition of this Culture Pattern states, we value collaborative individuals, but we simply don't value collaborative groups as much, and that is why so many organizations fail to achieve a culture of true collaboration. In our data, the contradiction here shows up in the scores around these three

---

2 Jamie Notter and Maddie Grant, *When Millennials Take Over: Preparing for the Ridiculously Optimistic Future of Business* (Ideapress, 2015), p.90.

Culture Building Blocks:
- Cross-functional communications
- Boundaries, borders, and territories
- Communication platforms

While Collaboration overall scores more futurist than average, and the three Building Blocks around collaborative individuals scored futurist at 4.12, these three Blocks around collaborative groups tell a different story. Combined, they scored only 3.49, ranking 11th out of the 16 pattern components. Cross-functional communications scored only 3.32, giving it a rank of 61 out of the 64 Building Blocks.

(Side note: for those of you into the numbers, we include all the Building Block scores and ranks for these patterns in Appendix B).

As much as we perennially complain about silos, it's interesting that the cross-functional communication piece is the most traditional here. The heart of cross-functional communication is proactive knowledge sharing—**do people in your organization make sure that people in other departments have the information they need in order to collaborate effectively? Most organizations don't, not because they are unable to communicate, but because people don't know how their work and the work of the other groups connect.**

So while this building block is within the culture marker of collaboration, it's rooted in a struggle around transparency. Remember, the competing commitment here is to subgroup autonomy, so **we're not creating systems where different groups proactively share what others need to know in order to collaborate effectively.** In *Humanize*, wea called this a culture of strategic transparency:

> A culture of transparency—of strategic transparency—
> [will] pull back the curtain in areas so employees, customers,
> or other stakeholders can get the information they need

to generate better results for the system.[3]

We found an example of this concept in action at Soles4Souls, a non-profit organization headquartered in Nashville, Tennessee, that turns donated shoes and clothing into opportunity, providing relief, creating jobs, and getting people out of the cycle of poverty. As their operation grew, they found themselves with an inventory of shoes and clothing that rivaled some major retailers in value. Hence, they needed to upgrade their inventory systems and implement enterprise resource planning (ERP) software, which is a tremendously complex task (that requires a lot of collaboration).

To layer in the right level of cross-functional transparency, they used software called Align (aligntoday.com) to make department-level priorities and tasks visible to everyone in the organization.

That broad visibility helped them excel at collaboration. When things got off track (as they inevitably do in a project like this), the conversation about getting back on track was clear and focused rather than angry and accusatory. Everyone was operating off of the same information, so they had the opportunity to proactively address issues when they could see one department falling behind on tasks.

"I'm stunned that a small organization like ours pulled that off in the way that we did," said Buddy Teaster, Soles4Souls CEO. He attributes much of the success to their ability to make the detailed lists of weekly tasks visible to everyone.

> You saw, we're at 40%, we should be at 60%. And it allowed
> us to have a conversation that wasn't, "Mike's an a******."
> It was more like, "What do we need to do to get back
> on track?" Having clarity around the goal was critical,
> but so were the details.

While cross-functional communication was the most traditional Culture Building Block in this Culture Pattern, the silo question—boundaries, borders, and territories—was only slightly more futurist, at 3.37 (compared to 3.32).

---

3 Notter and Grant, *Humanize* (2012), p. 161

The real problem with silos is not that boundaries exist; it's that those boundaries are not porous. It's okay to have silo boundaries to allow for deep work that requires deep expertise, but if those boundaries are too solid, where people outside the boundary cannot get enough access to the people or information they need to do their work, it slows progress and effectiveness. It's okay to maintain fences that divide our departments, but we need those fences to be two feet high so people can step over them when needed. Instead, most organizations maintain the symbolic version of 9-foot-high walls topped with razor wire.

The third building block related to our struggle with collaborative groups is focused on how (and if) we use our communication platforms. On the data side, most organizations are a little more futurist on this building block— it averages 3.75, which is above the overall average. But the high score can be deceiving, because we all know how this works: every department actively uses communication platforms, but frequently they each use a different one.

Some groups use Slack, others use Teams, and others do most of their communication in the project management system. Our teams embrace communication platforms, but we're not willing to bend our preferences so everyone is using the same one because that would enable better collaboration. This is the essence of Awkward Collaboration. Each group is continually frustrated that the other group hasn't heard what they've said.

Fortunately, Awkward Collaboration is not inevitable. Remember, you don't have to abandon the autonomy of subgroups. But you do have to find ways to reduce the desperate need for that autonomy, which enables collaboration among groups to happen more easily. The secret, it turns out, is in not pushing too hard.

How to Fix Awkward Collaboration

Getting groups to collaborate effectively is less about pushing people to collaborate more, and more about removing the obstacles to successful collaboration. You don't need everyone to be collaborating all the time—it's fine for groups to exist in your organization, and, yes, sometimes they are off in a corner by themselves getting stuff done. But for collaboration to be generative, where collaboration with your teammates happens as seamlessly as it does with other departments or levels in the hierarchy, **you must work hard to make cross-group collaboration easier.**

One organization that has done this well is the American Association of Endodontists (AAE), a nonprofit professional society headquartered in Chicago that serves as a global resource for endodontists (specialists in root canal treatments) and dental professionals. AAE is a small organization with about thirty staff and a $12 million annual budget. Like other associations, they hold a large annual conference and provide education, networking opportunities, and advocacy as they serve the profession. Success in that work requires collaboration, of course, and over the last few years, AAE has intentionally shifted its culture to maximize the effectiveness of their collaboration. There were two specific things that they did that serve as lessons for any organization that wants to eliminate the pattern of Awkward Collaboration:

- Reducing cognitive load, and
- Making hierarchy accessible.

Reducing Cognitive Load

In Bob Sutton and Huggy Rao's book, *Scaling Up Excellence*, they devote an entire chapter to cutting "cognitive load." Cognitive load refers to the limits of our mental capacity to deal with complexity. As the complexity of the work world grows, employees' ability to process all of it in their "working memory" declines, which, according to Sutton and Rao, "produces blind spots and bad decisions and saps their willpower."[4]

This has particularly bad implications for collaboration. Sutton and Rao cite one study where subjects were assigned to complete some simple structures using Legos, but some completed the task in groups of two while

---

4 Robert I. Sutton and Huggy Rao, *Scaling Up Excellence: Getting to More without Settling for Less* (New York: Crown Business, 2014), p. 99.

others did it in groups of four. While the quads were able to complete the task faster, on average, than the pairs, they weren't able to do it *twice* as fast, even though they had twice the person-power, which means they were ultimately less efficient. The cognitive load that is generated by communicating and coordinating with three people, as opposed to just one, takes its toll.

And that's just individuals collaborating with other individuals. When you add the layer of groups collaborating with groups, cognitive load can be even more of a challenge. Not only are you managing the cognitive load generated by collaborating among your own team members, you now must deal with the complexity of collaborating with people from other teams, who you may not know so well. That is why reducing cognitive load is so critical to defeating the Culture Pattern of Awkward Collaboration, and it's something that AAE tackled head-on in its culture change efforts.

They did this in several ways.

Decision-Making Role Clarity

Role clarity is critical if you want groups to collaborate effectively, specifically because it reduces the cognitive load around how people need to work together. In systems that lack role clarity, everyone on every project is doing mental calculations about who should be involved in the conversation, which slows them down. More importantly, cognitive energy is wasted in our maneuvering to try to keep people out of the decision-making process that we don't think "should" be involved.

AAE used the RACI model to clearly define decision-making roles. RACI stands for Responsible, Accountable, Consulted, and Informed. Each is a decision-making role that comes with specific responsibilities and expectations. For example, the R (responsible) is the decision maker, and the C (consulted) is someone that the R must consult for feedback before the decision is made. Yet many people don't realize that the R doesn't have to accept the C's advice. If they did—meaning the R and C must agree on the decision—then that C is actually just another R.

Once you get clear on those details, it reduces cognitive load. When I know my role is a C, then I can quickly give clear feedback on what I think works or doesn't work about the decision, and then I can let the rest of the process be managed by people in the other roles. (For a more detailed explanation of the RACI model, see Appendix C. This is one of the most popular culture plays in our playbook and you may find it particularly helpful.)

Project Management Reengineering

While role clarity was achieved at AAE relatively quickly and easily, their main effort to reduce cognitive load internally was to do a complete overhaul of their project management process. When they started this culture work, project management wasn't a glaring gap for them. "We were pretty good at project management," said Trina Andresen Coe, AAE's Deputy Executive Director. "But each team was doing it in their own way, and we realized that was making it harder when the projects required multiple teams."

But instead of just tweaking around the edges of project management to make it generically better—they went all in, investing in a new, comprehensive project management software system, combined with extensive training for all staff and process reengineering with the help of a consulting firm. It was a significant investment of time and money for an organization with such a small staff, but it has paid real dividends.

One of the small but powerful changes they made was a more disciplined approach to project kickoff meetings for their more complex projects. AAE runs a conference in the summer that has multiple events going on simultaneously over a weekend. Before the culture change initiative, the three people who handled the logistics would do a kickoff meeting, but now they have a standard process that involves everyone working all the events. That allowed them to solve problems proactively and develop creative new solutions. "It was really exciting," said Deb Brisson, Exhibit and Sponsorship Manager at AAE. "We ended up brainstorming some cool stuff about a new award we were giving out; that kind of conversation wouldn't have happened before."

More broadly, the new level of transparency that the project management system created had the effect of pulling back a curtain on an old way of working that had historically generated suspicion among the different departments. As Brisson noted,

> Before, we knew less about what was going on with each team in each department. When we would get a question, it spurned on more questions like, "Why do you need this?" You start thinking, how is this impacting me? What else don't I know? And what should I know? Why don't I know? It would just spiral. Now, because we're tuned in to what each department is working on, I can fill in a lot of those pieces myself.

When the proverbial veil is lifted, people spend less time making up stories in their heads about what happened or might happen—in other words, it greatly reduces cognitive load. That frees people up to become more quickly focused on exactly what needs to be done. In short, the new system immediately built trust, which is one of the four key capacities we explored in our book *Humanize*, and as you can see, one of its primary functions is to reduce cognitive load:

> Trust is a much more fundamental part of organizations than we tend to admit. The reason is that trust (and distrust, for that matter) is used by everyone to meet a critical need in the business world: It reduces complexity. The act of trusting someone or a group of people is powerful because it removes certain outcomes from your internal contingency planning. When you trust someone, you don't have to spend time figuring out how to protect yourself against the potential opportunities the other person has to take advantage of you… It allows you to get things done with increased speed and at lower costs.[5]

---

5 Notter and Grant, *Humanize* (2012), p. 156.

A key way they injected trust into their project management system was a standard process for getting senior management sign-off on any new project or significant addition to an existing project. If anyone wants to propose something new, they book time at the senior team's weekly meeting and make their pitch. The senior team asks and answers questions, hears their concerns, and ultimately either green-light the project or not. You may think this sounds like the top trying to control things, but it's really the opposite—they are trying to make it easier for staff at all levels to collaborate.

It is part of the broader "lifting of the veil" mentioned above. Now that everyone knows that all new projects have been approved by leadership, there is no longer any kind of suspicion or pushback when someone from another department is assigning you some tasks on the project management system. There is no more frustration that the other department isn't "doing their job" by asking you for help.

This is how increased trust translates into better results. The very act of "asking a question" at AAE has changed. Instead of being treated with suspicion, it is welcomed. People are happy to jump on a call to clarify an issue, no matter who brings it up. That means they solve problems faster, achieve better results, and make their customers and members happier.

While much of what they did was about detailed process engineering, CEO Ken Widelka knew from the beginning that this was more about culture change:

> There are interdepartmental project management and communication challenges in every organization. But the tools you use to manage projects are less important than changing the mindset and staff culture around how you do projects. This cultural approach helps ensure you clarify roles, leading to better projects and fewer conflicts.

Making Hierarchy Accessible

As you now know, the Awkward Collaboration Culture Pattern is based on the relative inability of groups to collaborate well (as opposed to individuals). While most people assume that means silos (and it does), it applies equally to groups distributed across your hierarchy. Hierarchy is about authority and control, so people sometimes don't view it as "collaboration," because of the power imbalances. But people with power imbalances collaborate all the time. It's not like the only reason you work together with your boss is because they could fire you (if that's the case, you should look for a new job). The quality of the collaboration really has nothing to do with the level of control or power either side has.

Remember, collaboration is about synergy—getting more out of the work the two parties do together than they could get done on their own. So, really, that puts more responsibility on the side that has more power. What can the powerful side do to ensure collaboration is synergistic? One key answer we found in our research with AAE was the simple act of making the upper rungs of the hierarchy more accessible to those below.

Many organizations believe their hierarchy is accessible and will cite their "open door" policy as evidence. But an open door is meaningless if people are afraid to go through it. **The physical barrier of the door is nothing compared to the relationship-based barriers in most organizations that keep people from crossing hierarchical lines to ensure better collaboration.**

Hierarchy is not only about decision-making authority and lines of supervision. As we rise in levels, we are given messages—some clear and some subtle—about how we will spend our time as we climb the ladder. Each level we reach gives us more access to those one level above us and implies spending less time with anyone below us. Then, our schedules fill up with meetings with our newly accessible colleagues, further reinforcing that we don't have time for people below us. It's almost unintentional, but after some time, the people lower in the hierarchy give up trying to reach out to people who are above them. With so little access, it starts to feel intimidating to attempt to reach out, hence the failed "open door" policies.

AAE, however, has done a great job at intentionally making their hierarchy more accessible. It starts with their overall mindset.

Speed Trumps Seniority

Creating an accessible hierarchy requires an overall mindset that values two things: speed and the inherent value of all employees. The speed part is fairly simple. In the AAE culture, the need to get things done quickly trumps any other rules about access across hierarchy lines. It doesn't change the decision-making authority, but people higher up will always take a meeting with someone lower when it will help move the project forward more quickly.

In more traditional organizations, it's the opposite. We ran a training program on managing generational differences in the workplace for a large healthcare organization several years ago. When we were discussing the Millennial generation, one of the managers told a story about an entry-level employee (a young Millennial at the time) who stopped one of the senior vice presidents as they passed in the hallway to ask them a question. In that culture, such behavior was considered outrageous. This is a large organization, so to get "face time" with the senior VP required going through their scheduler, and for that young Millennial, even that route was not guaranteed to result in a meeting.

That approach didn't make sense to the Millennial generation when they entered the workforce, who were heavily influenced by a society that had elevated the status of children when they were growing up. The family hierarchy was more rigid for Generation X and Baby Boomers (children should be seen, not heard), but Millennials interacted on a first-name basis with adults and routinely negotiated with them to solve problems.

Many felt that this child-centric approach would produce a Millennial generation that did not understand the rules of hierarchy, but that's not true. When Millennials were children, they knew full well that adults had the power. They didn't expect to be in charge. What they did come to expect, however, was access and influence, and when they entered the workforce, they were expecting the same.

That Millennial at the healthcare company wasn't planning on ordering the Senior VP around. They just wanted a chance to get an important question answered when they happened to be in the same place at the same time. And the benefit of having that conversation (rather than going through the scheduler) is speed.

AAE recognizes this and goes out of their way to make the senior level available to staff who need them. Kelsey Friedman is a coordinator in AAE's meetings department, and she appreciates how quickly things happen inside AAE's accessible hierarchy. "I have come from past workplaces that weren't like that, and you had to wait forever for a response. Whereas with AAE, if I need something answered to get it finished, everyone's willing to jump on a quick phone call and make sure that they are working with me to get the answers that I need."

The other part of the accessible mindset is a little more subtle, and it's about recognizing the inherent value that every employee brings to the table. People who are higher up in the hierarchy are usually the more experienced ones, so it's normal for them to have higher levels of knowledge or expertise. And while we don't often like to admit it, that can create a dynamic where senior people feel like they are wasting their time getting input or ideas from junior people.

Sure, sometimes it's not 100% efficient when someone with a more limited knowledge base is participating in the conversation. Given their lack of experience, they might occasionally suggest solutions that are not workable or move the conversation in a direction that is not productive. But here's where the mindset becomes important. Suppose you have several conversations with junior people where you felt they weren't bringing much value. In that case, you can experience a shift in your mindset, moving from a *conclusion* that their contribution wasn't helpful to a *belief* that they are unlikely to be of value in the conversation more generally.

There is a framework developed by management theorist Chris Argyris called the ladder of inference, and it explains how people observe things in the world, make sense of them in their head (by making assumptions and adding meaning), and then draw conclusions and take action. We use this tool when helping teams manage conflict more effectively, because going "down" the ladder (into assumptions and what data were observed) is usually key to finding a resolution to the conflict.

But it's also useful in maintaining an accessible mindset, because it identifies the difference between a conclusion and a belief. In the example above, you could observe contributions made by a junior staffer in some meetings and draw a conclusion that they don't have a lot to contribute, and then take the action of not inviting them to the next meeting. But let's say you had several other interactions with that junior person that confirmed your original conclusion—that they didn't have much to offer in a substantive meeting. When the confirmation is strong, your conclusion "graduates" to becoming a belief.

A belief is something you simply "know" is true, and unlike a conclusion, it's no longer based on observable data or a thought process on your end. In fact, one of the dangers of operating based on beliefs is that beliefs have a huge effect on what data you observe and remember to begin with. If there is a piece of data that contradicts your belief, your brain won't accept it. In other words, if, down the road, that junior staffer ended up having something really valuable to contribute during a meeting, your brain would ignore it, and you'd have no memory of it ever happening.

That may sound unbelievable, but it's been confirmed by early research on cognitive dissonance. Cognitive dissonance means holding two opposing ideas in your mind at the same time, and it creates psychological discomfort. Suppose you accept that smoking cigarettes causes cancer, for example, yet you decide to smoke regularly. In that case, these opposing ideas create dissonance, and your brain will find a way to resolve it to reduce the psychological discomfort. Smokers often do this by convincing themselves that they will quit soon. You know smoking is bad, but it's really just temporary, so it's okay right now—dissonance resolved.

But another way your brain can reduce the discomfort is to reject part of the dissonance altogether. In 1949, two Harvard professors ran an experiment where they showed subjects a sequence of five playing cards, but in each sequence, there was a "trick" card that had the wrong color based on the suit of the card (so a six of clubs would be red, or a queen of hearts would be black). At the beginning of the experiment, participants experienced "perceptional denial." In other words, when presented with a red six of clubs, they "saw" a black one.[6]

---

6 https://www.linkedin.com/pulse/red-spade-experiment-brendan-brown/ Accessed July 2023.

So yes, when that junior staff person makes a valuable contribution to the conversation, your brain can deny it or misinterpret it if that goes against a belief you've developed about that person. We have been in business meetings where someone makes a suggestion, but the team rejects the idea, only to have a different person (who is perceived to have more expertise) make essentially the same point and have it accepted by the team. You can imagine how difficult collaboration becomes if you're that person whose input is being consistently ignored.

If you are a woman reading this, you may be thinking "Um, yeah we've known about that one for a loooooong time." This happens so frequently to women in the workplace that there is a name for it: "he-peating." Coined by friends of an assistant professor at the University of Virginia, the definition states that "he-peating happens when a woman suggests an idea, gets ignored, then has the idea repeated by a man, under which circumstance the idea is absolutely adored."[7]

An antidote to this dynamic is intentionally building a mindset in your culture that everyone has something to offer. When that mindset is in place, when people who occasionally make contributions that aren't useful, those instances will remain as occasional exceptions to the general rule that everyone's opinion is valuable.

The way this shows up at AAE centers around an experience of respect in their culture. To be sure, we often roll our eyes at the claim of cultures based on respect. It's like honesty or integrity—these should be table stakes, and besides, respect can mean a lot of different things to different people. For AAE, however, it is specifically related to the idea that everyone can bring something to the table. This is how Cassandra Rotolo, Foundation Program Manager, puts it:

> "Everybody respects one another as individuals, as adults, as people. That makes collaborating so much easier than what I've experienced in the past. We all expect somebody,

7 https://www.dailydot.com/irl/hepeat-men-women-workplace/ Accessed July 2023.

everybody, to bring something to the conversation, to bring something to the project, whether it's experience, expertise, insight, whatever the case might be."

Even their project management system helps support the development of this mindset, because it makes everyone's contributions more visible, which can prevent individual conclusions from slipping into beliefs. "Our approach ensures that we are accountable," said CEO Widelka. "The task and project visibility encourages everyone on staff, and it keeps me from being the one slowing down a project. For me, it is also helpful to see all the work that is occurring that is not otherwise visible to me."

Project Approval and Culture Teams

Mindsets are a bit squishy and can be difficult to maintain, so if you really want to make your hierarchy more accessible, you'll need to build in some specific processes that will facilitate that. The concept here is simple: get the top and bottom of the system to work together directly.

This is a critical component of systems thinking, and it was advocated by one of the pioneers of systems thinking, Barry Oshry. Oshry created the "Power Lab," an intense, six-day residential workshop that helped leaders develop by exposing them directly to systems thinking.

In the Lab, participants enter a real-time simulation and are divided into three groups: elites, managers, and immigrants. The differences among the three groups in terms of power and resources are stark. The elites control pretty much everything, and the immigrants have very little. The managers are in the middle. In fact, those are the three main components of any system—tops, middles, and bottoms.

What's fascinating about the Power Lab is that regardless of who you put into each of those groups, they almost always act consistently with the expectations of those three systemic roles. If you put a bunch of CEOs into the immigrant group, they'll quickly start acting like bottoms, even though they are tops in real life.

The tops feel burdened by responsibility and the complexity of the system, so they end up holding on too tightly to control. Bottoms feel oppressed by the system (and specifically by the tops), and in that victim mode, they abdicate responsibility. Oshry calls this the "dance of the blind reflex." In most organizations, we fall into this dance unknowingly but consistently.

To transform this dance, the tops and the bottoms need a new relationship: partnership. Oshry defines partnership as "a relationship in which we are jointly committed to the success of whatever endeavor, process, or project we are engaged in."[8] Tops must work in partnership with bottoms to solve the organization's problems together. This rarely happens, however, and one of the causes, interestingly, is the third part of the system: middles.

If tops are burdened by responsibility and bottoms are oppressed by the system, the middles are torn between the two ends. They believe their job is to solve the problems of both the tops and the bottoms, but those two agendas conflict, making it very difficult for the middles to be successful. In their attempt to solve all the problems, they actually decrease the capacity for each end to do their own problem-solving. The result is frustration at all three levels, and burnout and sometimes a feeling of incompetence among the middles.

The solution is for middles to help facilitate problem-solving by the ends themselves. The middle can bring their unique perspective (they are the only ones who really see both sides) and tools to help each side resolve their issues.

That is precisely where processes for bringing the top and bottom together come in. At AAE, there are two key examples of processes that help the top and bottom of the organization be more in partnership, and we've already mentioned one of them: the new project approval process.

Project Approval

In the section above on Project Management, we mentioned a new process for getting approval on new projects or major changes to existing projects. Staff at any level (not just managers) make a pitch to the senior leadership team.

---

8   Barry Oshry, *Seeing Systems: Unlocking the Mysteries of Organizational Life*, 2nd edition (Oakland, CA: Berrett-Koehler Publishers, Inc, 2007), p. 85

Natalie Hughes is an Integrated Marketing Manager at AAE, and she recognizes that this specific process gives her access to information and perspectives that she would otherwise not have:

> Whenever I request a project, I'm going to attend the next executive team meeting, which I would never do and never get visibility into otherwise. I get to attend that meeting and present the project that I'm proposing in front of the executives of our company, and I get to answer their questions, field their concerns, and hear firsthand their reasoning about whether or not they would approve that project to move forward with the timeline that I'm suggesting.

Middle managers can still play a role in this process. They can help junior staff prepare for the meeting by sharing their perspectives on what the senior team might be focused on. They may have data or other resources they could provide that would make the pitch more effective. This is how you create an accessible hierarchy—the middle is facilitating and the top and bottom are working together to solve the issues.

Culture Teams

Another process that AAE used to make their hierarchy more accessible emerged out of the multi-year culture design work they did. After they completed their culture assessment, they created an internal culture team that would be tasked with analyzing the data and, ultimately, developing a list of change action items. We advised them to make that team as diverse as possible, both horizontally (across functions) and vertically (across lines in the hierarchy). We think this is just good practice for culture change—the broader the representation you have on the team, the easier it is to get buy-in for the changes they want to make down the road.

AAE agreed, so when they moved into implementation of the culture change action items, each "play" from their playbook that was implemented would be managed by another diverse working group. They had a diverse team managing that big project management overhaul, and they had another team working on developing their core values. The team that worked on core values added "as evidenced by" statements to each value to clarify how the values appear in AAE's workplace. For example:

- *Collaboration, as evidenced by a spirit of cooperation between staff and those that serve the specialty;*
- *Agility, as evidenced by adaptability in thought and action, and courage to implement change.*

Some might argue that core values should come from the top, but that's falling into Oshry's "dance of the blind reflex" and putting too much control at the top. If everyone is going to be living the values, then they should work together in partnership to develop them. The use of culture teams facilitated that.

How You Can Fix This Culture Pattern

Reducing cognitive load and making hierarchy accessible are two effective strategies for fixing the Awkward Collaboration pattern, and we've seen in the AAE case study some of the culture plays they used to address it, but they are not the only answers. As is the case with all of the Culture Patterns described in this book, you need to understand more deeply how the Culture Pattern applies to you and then design some specific interventions that will change your culture in a way that resolves the competing commitments. We summed it up in the subtitle of this book: see your hidden workplace patterns and get unstuck.

See Your Pattern

Your challenge will be to get under the surface of the Culture Pattern. Most cultures, as our research indicates, value collaborative individuals more than collaborative groups. Their commitment to collaboration is neutralized by a competing commitment to the autonomy of subgroups. But it's not enough to know that you have this Culture Pattern, you have to see very specifically where it is causing friction. Try to pinpoint the areas with the biggest negative impact on your results:

- Are you leaving money on the table because departments work in isolation and miss opportunities to collaborate?
- Do departments compete for control, intentionally withholding information to give themselves an advantage?
- Are the projects that end up behind schedule and over budget also the ones that have too much involvement by the senior level?
- Is middle management clinging to control rather than facilitating forward action?

Keep asking questions like this until you've identified the most prominent examples of culture friction. Start with the places where frustration happens. What's the cause of that frustration, specifically when it comes to collaboration? That will be your guide for figuring out what needs to change to improve your culture.

Get Unstuck

In Chapter 6 we give you our playbook model for culture change. Your challenge will be to come up with the right mix of plays, both quick wins and major projects, that will address your areas of culture friction. Each play will fall into one (or more) of six categories: process, structure/design, technology, talent/HR, rituals/artifacts, and stewardship.

In this chapter, we highlighted several plays that AAE ran in order to fix the pattern of Awkward Collaboration:

- Establishing role clarity using the RACI model [process, structure/design]
- New project management system [process, technology]
- Project greenlighting process to make hierarchy more accessible [process]
- Cross-functional culture teams [structure/design]

But that's just the beginning. Here are some plays other organizations have used to address the Awkward Collaboration pattern.

- **Cross-Department Help Process.** Develop and implement a formal process for requesting cross-departmental help. [process]

- **Department mash-ups.** Two departments matched up for an afternoon of collaboration and team building. [structure/design]

- **Staff buddy of the month.** Create a shadowing program to randomly pair staffers from different departments to discuss/share their work; shift buddies monthly. [process]

- **Online Organization Chart.** Create an accessible organization chart for employees to reference the different departments and a short summary of the work product and personnel in each department. [technology]

- **Shout-Out Program.** Build a staff shout-out program to highlight cross-departmental successes. [process[

- **Conflict Management Protocol.** Develop written procedures/policies to include in the employee handbook. [process]

- **Training in Meeting Facilitation.** Train staff on planning and facilitating effective meetings. [talent/HR]

Can you think of other culture plays that would work for you? Go to culturechangemadeeasybook.com where you'll find a place to browse more plays and submit your own ideas and experiments.

Wait... We know what you're thinking:

> You said this was going to be easy.
> But this feels... difficult. And complicated.
> And involving more people than just me.
> Aaagh... * stress *

Don't stress. Remember that "culture change made easy" isn't about avoiding hard work—it's about making the hard work pay off more quickly. In Chapter 6 we have a full model for culture change, and you may want to skip forward to that chapter right now, so you understand what it's going to take to make the change happen. It might make you feel better. Then come back to Chapter 3 on Lagging Transparency with a clearer head.

Lagging Transparency

BOTTOM LINE

Organizations that suffer from Lagging Transparency value reactive transparency more than they value proactive transparency.

- We excel at creating cultures where people are willing to share information with each other, when asked. Trust matters, and we work hard to make sure the information we share is meaningful and credible.
- We struggle, however, with creating systems and processes that share information proactively. We rarely share information by default and leaders are not as good at sharing the "why" behind tough decisions.
- The organizations with this Culture Pattern have a commitment to information sharing that is neutralized by a competing commitment to maintaining control over the information. They care about transparency, but it happens both too little and too late. They force

themselves to make decisions based on incomplete or even inaccurate information.

The problem with this Culture Pattern is that it creates knowledge gaps that lead to poor decisions.

- When employees at all levels can't get access to the right information at the right time, customers are frustrated, and colleagues end up falling short of their potential.
- The blanket commitment to "sharing information" masks the problem, so we end up settling for slower and poor-quality decisions.

The solution to this problem is to build a transparency architecture, clarify strategic success drivers, and double down on meeting employee needs.

- Our case study organization created a culture that supports proactive transparency partly by investing in a powerful intranet, making much more information available to everyone.
- They also go out of their way to make the firm's strategies, priorities, and metrics crystal clear to everyone, which enables more forward-thinking solutions at all levels.
- They accept the responsibility of building internal capacity and smoothing the path for employees to be successful so they can take advantage of the proactive transparency.

How you can solve it:

- See your pattern: identify the specific areas where culture friction is messing with success, like data not being accessible because departments have them locked down, or wasted effort because people don't understand the strategic priorities.
- Get unstuck: run culture plays like running 360 reviews or making KPIs visible to everyone.

Would You Tell Your Employees How Much You Make?

Jeff Wald is the CEO of Pinion, an accounting firm with about 600 employees. A few years ago, he was attending a meeting of all the senior associates in his firm and offered an "ask the CEO anything" session for them. At some point during the session, someone shouted from the back of the room, "How much money do you make?"

Without hesitation, he told them.

There was almost a startled silence in the room as people processed the information, and during that lull, Wald got out his phone and started composing an email. When asked what he was doing, he explained that he was sending an email to all the Partners telling them how much he gets paid. "Even my Partners don't know how much I get paid," he said, "so I'd rather them hear it from me, than from one of you."

Stories like this scare a lot of people. Salary, in particular, is a hot button, and the overwhelming majority of organizations keep that information private (as does. Pinion, in fact, outside of that one moment). But that moment is important, and it begs a question: What would you have done if you'd been surprised by that question?

Our bet is you would deflect. You'd explain that organizational policies prevent you from disclosing, or, if that weren't the case, you might chalk it up to "most organizations" not disclosing that information. If you were prepared, you might even cite a salary benchmarking study, explaining that you were within an appropriate range. And an answer like that is perfectly fine. It's honest, and few in the room would be surprised or upset by it. But the important question is, why would you choose to deflect? Why wouldn't you just tell people, like Wald did?

To put it more bluntly, what are you afraid of? You might worry that people inside your organization would disapprove of how high your salary is. Or perhaps you'd worry that this information would leak outside your organization. Maybe clients would find out and disapprove. If enough people were displeased by that information, it could pressure you to reduce your salary, which might be a disappointing outcome for you. By sharing your salary information, you would be taking a risk that could produce a bad outcome.

Wald, of course, was faced with that same risk, yet he chose to share the information anyway, because with risk comes reward. **True cultures of transparency will share information even if it feels risky. There is a limit to that maxim, of course, but cultures of transparency take the risks of sharing information because they want the rewards: increased speed, better decisions, and fewer missed opportunities.**

In *When Millennials Take Over,* we showed how the software company Menlo Innovations achieved better decision-making by being radically transparent. We also told the story of how General Stanley McChrystal transformed intelligence operations during the war in Iraq, going from 18 operations per month to 300 operations per month, by shifting the culture to transparency. And in *Humanize* we told the story of how Whole Foods became more adaptable to changing market conditions by (you guessed it) sharing salary and bonus data internally. The rewards of a culture of transparency are real and well documented.

The Problem: Lagging Transparency

Unfortunately, the average organization fails to reap the rewards of radical transparency. **While most cultures value transparency and information sharing at a high level, they are frequently not as intentional or strategic as they need to be in their commitment to internal information sharing.** They tolerate constant gaps in knowledge and information, and results suffer. Here is how it shows up inside organizations:

- Customer inquiries are too frequently met with, "I don't know, but I'll find out and get back to you."
- By the time the other department gets you the information you need, you've missed the opportunity to act.
- Trust erodes because no one can see what other people are working on all day

- Decisions are consistently made without the right information in hand
- Change is excessively hard because of the effort it takes to get everyone on the same page

This is what Lagging Transparency looks like in the real world. Organizations are committed to sharing information internally, but they haven't learned how to do it proactively. As a result, they are slower, they make less effective decisions, and they struggle with change, all of which contribute to them not reaching their potential and sometimes losing their best people. Why? Because organizations with this pattern are not proactive enough.

What is Lagging Transparency?

Organizations with the Lagging Transparency Culture Pattern value reactive transparency more than they value proactive transparency.

In other words, if individuals ask someone for information, they are happy to share it, but these organizations don't put in systems and processes to make sure that information is already in people's hands before they even think of asking for it.

Like all Culture Patterns, it is rooted in a competing commitment. **In this case, the commitment to information sharing is solid, but it is neutralized by an equally strong commitment to** *maintaining control over the information.* We still believe knowledge is power, and we are hesitant to distribute it without knowing how it will be used. Being careful with sensitive information is important, but if this competing commitment is not managed, the lack of transparency can slow things down.

When you try to control things, you inevitably move more slowly. Organizations with this pattern try to be transparent, but when people get the information they asked for, it's often too little too late. They force themselves to make decisions based on incomplete or even inaccurate information.

The aggregate data from our culture assessment reveals the pattern clearly. Employees across the board report that things like "knowledge sharing," "trust," and "information credibility" were generally solid components of the culture, but all of those are about sharing information reactively, e.g. when someone asks for it. But the questions that focused on sharing information proactively ("information quantity," "information availability," and "hard truths") were not as present. This pattern, it turns out, can be a big problem.

How Lagging Transparency Shows Up: Knowledge Gaps

Part of the challenge of Lagging Transparency is "you don't know what you don't know." We share information every day. If anything, based on the number of meetings in everyone's schedule, one could argue that we're sharing too much. Sometimes, we get overwhelmed by the information being thrown at us, so it seems counter-intuitive to suggest we need to share more information earlier on.

But despite all the information sharing, we are routinely operating with important gaps in our knowledge. Knowledge gaps are quite common inside organizations because we're not making information available BEFORE people need to ask for it. What if your salespeople had that information about the new product features before the customer called to ask them about it? What if your different divisions all saw the shift in the market early and were able to adjust their strategies ahead of the competition? Frequently, those opportunities are lost, because organizations suffer from the Lagging Transparency pattern.

We see this all the time around setting strategic goals and targets. The management team will identify annual goals for the organization, and they will do a good job of sharing the strategy with everyone in the company. They may even have visible dashboards in the office as reminders about the progress the organization is making (or not making) against those targets.

But those are lagging indicators. We only really know if we hit our targets at the end of the year. In addition to the lagging indicators, we need to get better at leading indicators—metrics that will let us know we are off track while we still have an opportunity to change our tactics in order to hit the target.

Manufacturing and sales are two areas that are typically good at paying attention to leading indicators. Yes, sales teams will always track total units sold (lagging), but they also have their eyes further up the funnel, measuring the number of leads and qualified leads coming in, because if those numbers dip below a certain level, it requires an adjustment right away, otherwise they risk missing their sales quota at the end of the quarter. Similarly, manufacturing operations will track production schedules, inventory levels, materials usage, purchasing patterns, etc. in order to make the right strategic adjustments along the way. Without the leading indicators, adjustments would not be made until it's too late.

But outside of sales and manufacturing, traditional management didn't value that kind of proactive information sharing. The default was to report on things after the fact. Reporting is fine, of course, but if that's all you do, you'll suffer from knowledge gaps.

Knowledge gaps plague customer service as well. When customers reach out to one of your employees to get information or a question answered, it's quite possible that that employee will not know the answer or have the information requested, and that's okay. It's impossible for everyone to know everything. When this happens, the employee will give some version of "I don't know the answer to that, but I will find out and get back to you."

For example, imagine an employee of a trade association at the organization's annual meeting. An important member pulls them aside, because some important legislation has recently passed, and the member wants to know how the association is going to respond on Capitol Hill. The staff person in question is not part of the advocacy team, so they don't have any detailed knowledge about how the advocacy team plans to respond. From a basic customer service point of view, it makes sense to respond with, "Well, that's not my department, so I don't have the answer, but give me your card, and I will have someone on the advocacy team reach out to you right away."

The problem emerges when that kind of answer becomes frequent. Your employees are probably operating with significant knowledge gaps, whether it's about what another department is doing, how one of your products or services has changed, or what's happening in the marketplace that will directly impact your business. The example above is nonprofit-specific, but it could just as well have been a customer asking why a feature had been removed from the latest product update or even an internal customer asking an employee in the marketing department about the status of their social media campaign. When "I don't know but I'll get back to you" becomes a common answer, customers lose faith.

And when customers lose faith, they tend to stop being customers. The member starts questioning the dues they've been paying to an association that doesn't seem to be on top of such an important legislative issue. The customer stops calling you with product questions and ends up looking on the internet, where they get bombarded by ads for your competition. Your colleague gives up on contacting the marketing department for updates and starts considering side-stepping the department altogether and running the social media campaign on their own.

If you could fix the Lagging Transparency pattern, the interactions would look very different. That employee at the conference is never going to know all the details of the legislative response the association was planning, but if they had at least some visibility into the activities of the advocacy team, then their response to that member inquiry could mention that the advocacy team had been meeting on that issue just last week. They still would need to get back to the member with more details, but the member would leave the interaction with more faith that the association was, in fact, on top of this important issue.

The same would be true in the other examples. That customer would be content to wait on the details if the first person they reached could provide the explanation as to why the product change was made. That program staff would not lose faith in the marketing department if the marketing employee could provide at least a rough timeline for the social media campaign and was quick to make the connection with the people in the marketing team who had more details.

That is why you need to fix the pattern of Lagging Transparency in your culture. Operating with knowledge gaps prevents you from reaching your potential. But to fix the pattern, you must have a deeper understanding of how it works inside your culture.

Breaking the Pattern Down: Reactive Transparency v. Proactive Transparency

Like all Culture Patterns, there is one part where we excel and one where we struggle. **For transparency, the difference lies in being reactive versus proactive.**

Where We Excel: Reactive Transparency

In traditional management, information was shared on a "need to know" basis only. It was controlled from the top. Traditional management was engineered for efficiency, so putting too much information in the hands of too many people would be a distraction or cause confusion.

Today, most organizations have moved away from that approach, at least a little. In our aggregate culture assessment data, Transparency scores 3.60 out of 5, which is well above the traditional line of 3.00, but it is below the overall average of 3.69. In fact, among the eight Culture Markers, only Agility scored lower, at 3.52, so the evolution away from traditional management is less here than in the other areas. That said, Transparency follows the same pattern as all of the Culture Markers, with three of the specific Building Blocks showing up as more futurist than the rest. They are:

- Trust
- Information credibility
- Knowledge sharing

Those three combined averaged 3.83, which is above the average, though not quite futurist. These Building Blocks represent the foundation for an organization that values transparency. **Most organizations have a baseline level of trust that makes information sharing effective, and the information they are sharing is, on the whole, believable and meaningful to people.** Very few organizations have stayed with the "need to know" approach to information sharing. If people ask, we share the information. If you're someone known for hoarding information, it could get you in trouble or possibly moved out of the organization.

If you do reactive information sharing well in your culture, **you will have created an environment where the levels of competency are high enough that basic levels of trust are rarely questioned**. There won't be incessant double-checking or repeated end runs in order to avoid those people who can't be counted on to perform. When this level of trust is in place, it's much easier to take the risk (as we mentioned at the top of the chapter) of sharing information. Less risk means more information gets shared.

Similarly, you will also have put in place a basic level of competency when it comes to internal and external communications. When leadership announces something to staff, it won't be greeted with eye-rolls and post-meeting hallway conversations filled with outrage and sarcasm. That's not to say everyone agrees with what leadership has to say all the time, but the information shared internally is generally believable and meaningful. Establishing this baseline of credibility reduces cognitive load and frees people up to work more efficiently.

Most importantly, **your people are open to sharing information with their colleagues.** Information flow may not be perfect, but the gaps are not based on any kind of suspicion that sharing information will come back to haunt people. Your people rarely get defensive about sharing information because it is outside of normal job duties. If they have the information, they have no problem sharing it.

But note that all of this information sharing is done reactively. We tend to wait for people to ask for something before we share the information. Being proactive with information, however, is a different story.

Where We Struggle: Proactive Transparency

In *Humanize*, we told the story of a financial planning organization that had implemented a "transparency architecture," where key financial, strategic, and operational information was shared with all the financial planners in the company.[1] This is the opposite of sharing information on a "need to know" basis. They couldn't predict how and when the planners would use the information, but they assumed that getting more information out to them proactively would enable better decisions making. And if it's any indication, their turnover rate dropped from 23% to 11% after making the change.

But that kind of proactive system for information sharing is the exception today, rather than the rule. It turns out there is a piece of traditional management that many organizations continue to hold onto, even if it doesn't always serve them, and that's control. In mechanical systems (the basis of traditional management), all the inputs are carefully controlled and introduced at exactly the right time in the process in order to produce the expected result. There is no need to proactively provide an input (like information) until its appointed time in the process. In fact, letting that get out of your control feels dangerous.

The same is true with information sharing today. We're better at reactive information sharing because it feels safer to give that discrete bit of information that is requested—it feels like there are fewer ways it might go sideways. It's like you're handing them the one puzzle piece they are missing. Proactive information sharing, on the other hand, would be more like dumping the puzzle pieces onto the table at the beginning. It feels messy—and risky.

So it is no surprise that the scores in the aggregate data around proactive transparency are noticeably more traditional than the three reactive transparency Blocks. The proactive Blocks include:

- Information quantity
- Hard truths
- Information availability

These three Blocks combined averaged only 3.38, tied for 15th in the list, meaning only one pattern component scored lower than this one. *Hard truths* and *information availability* individually ranked 59 and 60 out of 64. These elements are simply not very present in most cultures today.

---

1 Notter and Grant, *Humanize* (2012), p. 161.

Information quantity **is the heart of proactive transparency. It's about creating systems and processes that make sure more information is flowing to more people.** When these systems and processes are in place, instead of needing to ask people for the information, they already have the information before they even realize they need to ask. The *information availability* Building Block is related. Organizations that score high on this block believe that information should by default be made public unless there is a reason to keep it private. These are both about making sure that information is out there BEFORE it's needed.

The *hard truths* Building Block is about how well the senior level in the organization is communicating about the tough decisions they must make, and why they made them. This is a data point that usually shows some difference (unsurprisingly) across the levels in the organization. If you ask the senior level, they feel like they do a pretty good job at communicating about the tough decisions. The people below them, however, often feel like they are left too much in the dark.

At the heart of our struggle with proactive transparency is fear. Think back to the story at the top of this chapter—you probably would be hesitant to share your salary number with employees. Why? Because you'd be afraid that it would make some people upset. The safer choice is to say nothing—to control the information—in order to avoid a negative outcome. That thought process enters into more information-sharing opportunities than you might think.

When leadership needs to make a strategic shift or make changes to a major program, they often wait as long as they can to share the information because they are afraid of how various employees or groups will react or interpret their decisions. They will wait until they can iron out more of the details before sharing anything. In the end, though, that doesn't change the reactions they are going to get, other than to add some frustration based on how last-minute people are learning about the decision.

How to Fix Lagging Transparency

Breaking the Lagging Transparency pattern requires strategic information sharing. It's not about sharing all the information all the time—that would be overwhelming. **It's about learning how and when to share the right information earlier in order to enable better decision-making.**

The case study for how to overcome the pattern of Lagging Transparency was actually introduced to you at the top of this chapter: Pinion, whose CEO boldly shared his salary information with his Senior Associates. As a professional services firm, Pinion specializes in the food and agriculture industry and has 26 offices in 11 states across the U.S. Over the last ten years they have grown extensively through acquisition of other firms, and they have recently expanded their presence internationally as well.

As a firm, their commitment to transparency is intentional and driven from the top, particularly since Wald became the CEO ten years ago. The leadership realized that they had been spending a lot of time trying to determine what should be shared and what shouldn't. As you might expect, not everyone sees eye to eye on that issue, so the conversations can take a lot of time, and it was creating a drag on effectiveness. In addition, like many organizations, the employees had developed an underlying suspicion of what was happening "behind the curtain." So they decided to make a radical shift:

> The default is that everything will be shared, unless there
> is a reason to keep it private.

They knew there were certain pieces of information that would not be shared, but beyond that, everything was public. As a result, employees soon realized that there really wasn't a significant curtain hiding anything. "We found when we flipped it that there really wasn't that much, honestly, that we could not share totally publicly with people in the firm," said CEO Jeff Wald. "It really changed people's attitude in terms of their relationship with what's going on in the firm and what's going on behind the scenes."

More than just reducing suspicion, they realized that the increased transparency was instrumental in driving the success of both employees and the organization as a whole, and it was equally important in supporting their ability to be agile and innovative.

But defeating the Lagging Transparency Culture Pattern requires more than merely taking the stance that information is public by default. Pinion did it by focusing on technology, strategy, and people:

- Building the Transparency Architecture (technology)
- Sharing the Why (strategy)
- Focusing on Employee Needs (people)

Building a Transparency Architecture

In *When Millennials Take Over*, we wrote a case study on Menlo Innovations, a software company in Ann Arbor, Michigan. Part of their information-sharing infrastructure is a project management system that is visible to everyone. They work in pairs at Menlo, so every week each pair will have 40 hours' worth of tasks planned, and these tasks (and the progress being made) are visible to everyone else all the time.

The CEO is not exempt from this system—everyone can see if he is ahead or behind on his weekly tasks. But where it becomes truly useful is when people fall behind. Since everyone can see everyone else's progress, people can make their own decisions about when to stop their work and go help someone else. This didn't require a supervisor to manage that, it didn't require a bunch of boring status update meetings, and it didn't even require a string of emails back and forth.

At Menlo, when you want to communicate with team members, you use what they call "high speed voice technology." All 50 employees work in one large room, so if we were Menlo employees and wanted to have a meeting with Rich Sheridan, the CEO, we would simply say "Hey Rich" in his direction, and when he responds with "Hey Jamie and Maddie," then suddenly we're having a meeting, and can solve whatever problems we need to. Not one email needs to be sent.

It's kind of ironic that a software company relies on such analog methods of communication. In fact, their project management system is not software at all—it's made up of sheets of paper, string, and sticky dots, and it exists on the back wall of the room where they work. Everyone can see it, and everyone knows what the different colored dots mean in terms of status, so everyone instantly has the information they need to make smarter, more effective decisions.

Of course, Menlo is only 50 people, and the nature of their work is conducive to their working all together in one room. Pinion, on the other hand, has offices spread across the world, so they are unable to copy Menlo's innovative solution. With the recent explosive growth of remote work everywhere, even small organizations would have a hard time employing the sticky dot system today, which means most organizations must rely on technology to be the backbone of their transparency architecture.

That's where a good intranet comes in. Pinion invested in a robust intranet, including a comprehensive set of dashboards for the firm, back in 2019. It was an initiative led by their Director of Internal Communications, Debra Helwig. The intranet includes updated quarterly goals for the whole firm, broken down by work stream. It includes information on their recent merger and acquisition activity. It includes information on which service lines are being added or shut down. As Helwig noted, "If you have the desire to go and look, you can find it…"

> …If you want to know what the financial performance of the firm is, you can go to the firm dashboard from the homepage of the intranet and at any time and drill down by market and drill down by function as to how our performance is in various areas. We publish very clearly who the leaders are in all of our markets and all of our functions.

That is what a true transparency architecture looks like, and they complement the digital flow of information with other forms of communication as well. Quarterly they do what they call "meeting in a box" (since it's done by Zoom), which is an all-hands meeting where critical information is shared directly with staff (rather than only making it available on the intranet, which they also do, of course). It's not just senior leadership broadcasting the party line. It includes leaders at all levels sharing their goals and what they're doing to accomplish them, even when things are not going so well.

In fact, that is one of the aspects of a transparency architecture that is often overlooked—it requires some conversations that are not so comfortable. The dashboards that are on their intranet will show some individuals' goals, progress, and other KPIs. As People Officer Christina Ricke noted,

> It has their new solutions goal, their revenue managed goal, their personal productivity goal, their gross margin realization, etc. Those are out there, and anybody can see anybody else's dashboard. You can look it up anytime. That can generate some tough conversations, so you also have to invest in good leadership and communication skills training if you're going to be super transparent because you need to equip more people with how to productively navigate conversations like that.

When you combine the skill development, the technology infrastructure, and the intentional all-staff communications, you have the potential for huge productivity gains. Pinion recently acquired a large firm, and they leveraged their transparency architecture to make sure the acquisition was a success.

Kendra Moran was part of the acquired firm, and she could see clearly how the culture at Pinion supported a successful integration of the two firms:

> We had a lot of integration meetings going into the merger, and a key ground rule was put out there: if you don't speak up, then you're accepting what's going on, and you need to go with it. Once the merger did happen, I think that mindset really helped because if something's not right, it opened up that door to speak up. And it hasn't been confrontational. Everybody just says, okay, what is the pain point? There's more give and take and finding a mutual spot on what we're trying to implement so that it benefits all of us.

According to an article in Harvard Business Review,[2] 70 to 90 percent of all acquisitions fail—yet Pinion has been remarkably successful, in large part due to their focus on full transparency. This is where you start to see the true ROI of improving your culture.

Sharing the Why

In addition to their transparency architecture, another way that Pinion achieves proactive transparency is through their disciplined strategic clarity. We've already pointed out that they share company goals and KPIs on their intranet, and this kind of strategic visibility is important for leveraging the potential behind proactive transparency. In fact, that same visibility was mentioned in the previous chapter on collaboration, with the example of the nonprofit SolesforSouls making multiple layers of goals and progress towards those goals visible across the organization to enable more effective collaboration.

But strategic clarity goes deeper than sharing your KPIs across the board. As Simon Sinek has famously pointed out, it "starts with why." In Sinek's widely viewed TED talk from 2014, he laid out his "golden circle" model with three concentric circles, starting with "why" in the center, "how" in the next ring out, and "what" in the outermost ring. He argued that nearly everything we do and say, both as individuals and organizations, tends to work from the outside in. We start with what, then move to how, and only in some instances do we even address the why.

The what is the clearest to us—this is what we do, the products or services we provide, or the concrete, logical answers. The how might be some of the specific features or benefits that differentiate our product or ideas, and the why is our core purpose, our beliefs that drive what we're doing, to begin with.

---

2 Graham Kenny, "Don't Make this Common M&A Mistake," *Harvard Business Review*, March 16, 2020, https://hbr.org/2020/03/dont-make-this-common-ma-mistake# Accessed August 2023.

The why is the most fuzzy, according to Sinek, which explains why we don't like to start with it. Despite the fuzziness, he argues that starting with the why is more effective, because it connects to our limbic brains, which have a greater impact on our behavior than the more logical neo-cortex. The neo-cortex focuses on the outer circle of what.

He gave the example of Apple, a company that doesn't market its computers by explaining what great computers they have to offer, and then talking about how they are beautifully designed, simple to use, and user-friendly. Instead, he argued, they do it like this:

WHY: Everything we do, we believe in challenging the status quo; we believe in thinking differently.

HOW: The way we challenge the status quo is by making our products beautifully designed, simple to use, and user friendly.

WHAT: We just happen to make great computers...wanna buy one?[3]

When people connect with the why, the how and what become more important to them, and that is what triggers behavior changes (in this case, buying computers). By connecting with why first, it can also lead to other behaviors, like buying MP3 players, smart phones, tablets, etc. Other computer companies also attempted to expand into those other product lines, but they were ultimately less successful, Sinek argues, because they didn't start with why.

This is a very deep form of proactive transparency. **The purpose of proactive transparency is to enable better decision-making. Systems that rely on reactive transparency settle for incomplete pictures, with lots of gaps in their knowledge.** People in those systems then have to take time to ask other people for that information to fill the gaps, but in today's hectic environment, they may not have the time to do that, so they fill in the gaps with their own assumptions. In other words, they make it up.

When we don't share the why with our people, we are asking them to invent it for themselves, and what they invent is not only wrong, it's more

3   https://www.ted.com/talks/simon_sinek_how_great_leaders_inspire_action?
    language=en Accessed August 2023.

often rather uncharitable. It's easy for us to assume that Apple sells its computers only because it wants to maximize profit, or, in the case of Pinion, that it is pursuing growth through the acquisition or adoption of a particular compensation structure simply to line the pockets of the partners.

Pinion doesn't let that happen, however, because they are good at explaining the why. At the highest level, they have a "massive transformational purpose" that explains their deeper beliefs about why they exist as a firm.[4] And it doesn't just sit on their website. They use their "meeting in a box" structure to make connections between the operations of the business and their massive transformational purpose on a quarterly basis. This is what makes this purpose more actionable. It becomes part of people's decision-making process.

But Pinion doesn't stop there. They work hard to ensure everyone in the organization is clear on the firm's strategy. There are two questions we ask in our culture assessment that focus on strategic clarity. One asks if employees are aware of their organization's strategy and use that awareness in their decision-making, and the second asks if they have a clear understanding of what truly drives the success of the organization at a deeper level.

Pinion scored above average on both. The first one—awareness of the chosen strategy of an organization—is within the transparency Culture Marker. Pinion scored 3.75 on a five-point scale, compared to the overall average of 3.59 for that question. This aspect of proactive transparency was discussed above in the technology section. Pinion uses their intranet, meeting in a box, and other processes to ensure that everyone in the organization is aware of the goals and strategies of the firm.

The second question goes a bit deeper and focuses on knowledge of the specific factors that drive the success of the organization. This question is not in transparency—it's in the Culture Marker of inclusion. **Whether or not everyone in your organization has a clear understanding of what drives the success of the enterprise is ultimately an issue of inclusion**

---

4 Massive Transformational Purpose is a term covered in Salim Ismail, Peter Diamandis, and Michael Malone, *Exponential Organizations 2.0* (Powell, OH: Ethos Collective, 2023).

rather than just communication/transparency. Organizations must choose: will they sequester that knowledge only at the top of the org chart, or will they work hard to make sure people outside of the leadership deeply understand what drives success?

Many organizations are hesitant about that choice, but not Pinion. They have built into their culture a tenacious focus on where they are headed and drive it down to the individual level.

Lance Woodbury is a Partner in the firm, and he explained that conversations about goals, roadmaps, and where both individuals and the firm are headed are constant:

> Where are you headed? What are your goals? What's your roadmap? I mean, that can get a little tiring, but it serves transparency. It supports transparency to constantly, say, be asking where we headed? Where are we going?

Ulises Gonzales is a recruiter at Pinion, and he refers to this approach as "future tense thinking."

> We're always thinking in the future tense. As a campus recruiter, I'm hiring for one or two years down the road. The "why" that I usually am looking for isn't why are we doing it today? It's more so, why are we doing it for two, three, four, even ten years down the road? We are looking ahead all the time. For me, it's super important to understand the why. It might not be necessary to explain that to an external audience, but for me to look for specific types of recruits, ones that can successfully integrate themselves into the firm a couple of years from now, it's critical.

We have always said, only half-jokingly, that people don't resist change—they resist doing things they think are stupid. They resist doing things that they believe go against their own interests. That is why explaining the why is so important.

Focusing on Employee Needs

In *When Millennials Take Over* we identified four key capacities that move organizations toward the future of work: digital, clear, fluid, and fast. We have already mentioned in this chapter the case study we used for clear, since that has an obvious connection to transparency. What might not be so obvious, however, is the connection between the Culture Pattern of Lagging Transparency and one of the other three capacities: digital.

Specifically, one of the most important aspects of digital is what we call the "digital mindset." Beyond the technology component of digital, the digital mindset requires an approach to the workplace using the same thinking that software designers use when creating software products, and that starts with a disciplined focus on the user.

As Gen Xers, the authors are old enough to remember version 1.0 of pretty much every software that people use today to get work done, and let's be honest: software back then was written based on the needs of the programmer, not the user. Very little of it was intuitive, which is precisely why you needed a 300-page manual to come in the box with the floppy disks that contained the software. If you couldn't figure out how to add a footnote, then you would just look up "footnote" in the index of the manual, and find the proper instructions for completing the task.

Software today doesn't come with a manual (or hardware, for that matter). Part of that is because the internet has become our manual, of course, but beyond that, software has been intentionally designed to be much more user-focused. Even though we use different devices and have different contexts, none of us needs a manual, because the operations we're completing already make sense to us. It's intuitive.

Our case study for the digital mindset in that book was a small nonprofit, and the users they were focused on were their employees. They designed their office to enable every individual to work almost exactly as they wanted to. They customized job descriptions for every employee every year. If something required more work by the organization in order to make it easier for the employee, that's what they did. The employees are the users of that culture, so the culture was designed around their needs.

So what does this have to do with transparency? Our research at Pinion revealed a link, and it revolves around this simple but important concept:

With transparency, comes responsibility.

The purpose of proactive transparency is to put information in the hands of your people, so they can take smarter actions and make better decisions. That means you must make sure that (a) they have the capacity to act and make good decisions, and (b) their environment isn't getting in the way of them doing that. It's like tending to the soil before planting your seeds.

For proactive transparency to be effective, your culture must place a heavy emphasis on meeting employee needs. There are two components to that: (1) building employee capacity, and (2) continuous improvement to make employees more successful.

Building Employee Capacity

Proactive transparency gives people permission to act, so the organization has the responsibility to build the capacity of those people to act effectively.

The whole point of proactive transparency is that people can take action and make better decisions based on the information that is now in front of them. As we mentioned above, the employees at Menlo Innovations can see everyone's project status, so they make their own decisions about when to stop their work and move to help someone else.

In order to make that effective, Menlo also built a strong culture of feedback and learning. Their performance review system is simple: when you want feedback on your performance, you buy lunch for your peers and they give you feedback. You can do this as often as you like, and while these feedback lunches can also be a part of your moving to a higher pay grade, their primary purpose is learning.

Menlo CEO Rich Sheridan quotes systems thinking pioneer Peter Senge in his second book: "In the long run, the only sustainable source of competitive advantage is your organization's ability to learn faster than your competition."[5] In addition to the feedback lunches, Menlo encourages all employees to read extensively (at the back of his book he provides a recommended reading list of more than 40 books to get you started).

Similarly, Pinion's culture has a strong emphasis on learning and employee development. We measure employee development in our culture assessment in the Building Block of *training and development* (it's in the Culture Marker of Growth). Specifically, it asks if the organization spends time and money giving its employees skills/knowledge they didn't have before they got there. In our aggregate data set, that specific block scores more traditional than most—3.35 on our 5-point scale, ranking 57th of 64 individual Building Blocks. Almost every organization we know has a training and development budget, but it's clearly not going as far as it could.

Pinion, on the other hand, scored a remarkable 4.08 on that Block. Pinion's scores were generally above the aggregate average, but no single Block had as much of a difference as the 0.73 gap on learning and development. It may have ranked 57th in the aggregate, but for Pinion it was 14th. Developing their people is a cornerstone of their culture, as Principal Kendra Moran explains:

> The way that they develop individuals along the way, from an intern all the way up to top, is unbelievable. I look at our younger staff and think, I'm excited for you all— you'll have a completely different level of education that you would have received in another firm.

And People Leader Christina Ricke ties this directly to proactive transparency:

> If you're going to invest in being transparent, you also better be investing in leadership and communication skills training, too. If you put transparency out there, but don't teach people

---

5 Richard Sheridan, *Chief Joy Officer: How Great Leaders Elevate Human Energy and Eliminate Fear* (New York: Portfolio/Penguin, 2018), p. 210.

how to live in it, that could actually, for a short window
of time, be worse than being more private in the first place.

Continuous Improvement

Developing individuals is only one part of the employee focus that proactive
transparency requires. Proactive transparency makes flaws visible, so the organization has the responsibility to continuously improve things to make sure
employees can be successful.

The upside of proactive transparency is that it makes information visible
and leads to better decisions and more effective actions, but there is a downside as well. When you shine a light on everything, you start seeing the aspects
of your organization that are messing with people's success.

No organization is perfect, and even the things that you have right today
are likely to become less effective as your environment morphs and changes.
In cultures that focus only on reactive transparency, those imperfections
can more easily be swept under the rug. If I wait for you to ask me to share information, I have the ability to shape and spin what I'm sharing, or I can simply
omit the parts that might reveal flaws. So we live with our imperfections,
and employees are forced to operate in an inefficient environment.

**If you want proactive transparency to work, then you must commit
to fixing the problems that are revealed.** You must focus on making things
easier for your employees, because that's the only way you'll get the real value
of the increased transparency. Unfortunately, not a lot of organizations will
embrace this commitment.

Part of overcoming this problem is embracing what Adam Grant calls
"confident humility." In his book, *Think Again*, Grant tackles one of the most
important parts of learning, both at an organizational and individual level:
being wrong. When you are wrong, or there are flaws, it presents an opportunity for rethinking things, which is when new and better solutions
are developed. As Grant explains, this is at the heart of scientific thinking:

> If you're a scientist by trade, rethinking is fundamen-
> tal to your profession. You're paid to be constantly aware
> of the limits of your understanding. You're expected to doubt

what you know, be curious about what you don't know, and update your views based on new data. In the past century alone, the application of scientific principles has led to dramatic progress. Biological scientists discovered penicillin. Rocket scientists sent us to the moon. Computer scientists built the internet.[6]

At the heart of scientific thinking lies confident humility—"having faith in our capability while appreciating that we may not have the right solution or even be addressing the right problem."[7] This requires maintaining an appropriate balance between the belief you have in yourself and the belief you have in your tools.

The belief you have in yourself is basic self-confidence—knowing that you are up to the task. If your confidence is too low, then it won't really matter how competent you are, you'll suffer from impostor syndrome, and fail to take action. If your self-confidence is too high, however, you can start to lose sight of your actual competence level and end up saying or doing things that ultimately don't make sense (armchair quarterback syndrome).

The belief you have in your tools is your attachment to the specific conclusions or solutions that you are employing at any given moment. If you are fundamentally unsure of your solutions it has the same effect as low confidence—your doubt can lead to inaction. But if you are overly sure of your specific answers, it can lead to arrogance that can ultimately steer you in the wrong direction.

Grant simplifies it into a 2x2 matrix, where your belief in yourself is either secure or insecure, and the belief in your tools is either certain or uncertain. Confident humility combines a secure belief in yourself with an uncertain belief in your tools. You know that you can do it, but you also know that your current answers probably need to be improved.

---

6 Adam Grant, *Think Again: The Power of Knowing What You Don't Know* (New York: Viking, 2021), pp. 19-20.

7 ibid. p. 47.

One of the biggest challenges is maintaining that balance as your competence improves. As Grant explains,

> As we gain experience, we lose some of our humility.
> We take pride in making rapid progress, which promotes
> a false sense of mastery. That jump-starts an overconfidence
> cycle, preventing us from doubting what we know and being
> curious about what we don't. We get trapped in a beginner's bubble of flawed assumptions, where we're ignorant
> of our own ignorance.[8]

So, in addition to putting in systems and processes to make information more proactively available, Pinion has built a culture that embraces confident humility and expects solutions to be continuously improved. As much as they are committed to quality and effectiveness, they never let that slide into a desire for perfection, which can be the enemy of proactive transparency, as Principal Becky Sweet explains:

> We can't ever expect a perfect process. I think that "being
> real" is a big piece of transparency. I know that some things
> aren't perfect with this or aren't right yet, and we're still figuring it out—but you know we're figuring it out.

And this all ties back to training and development and strategic clarity. By being diligent about communicating the firm's strategy and success drivers, Pinion's culture can generate that baseline confidence—that feeling of "we got this." If that strategic information were not visible, employees, particularly at the lower level, might slip into impostor syndrome, feeling like someone at their level wouldn't have the right knowledge to take action. But as Manager Kristin Zerger explains, that is not common at Pinion:

> The key is knowing where you're headed, knowing what
> the end goal is, but maybe not being sure how we're going

---

8 ibid. p. 45.

to get there. I think that's the fun part—leaving a lot of it to me, even with me not knowing the "middle," but getting to figure out how to do it and testing along the way, not being afraid to fail.

Combining strategic clarity with developing people's capacity and confident humility leads to the continuous improvement that proactive transparency needs in order to be successful.

How You Can Fix This Culture Pattern

Building a transparency architecture, sharing the why, and focusing on employee needs are three good ways to transform the Lagging Transparency pattern, but your needs may vary. Here is how to start seeing your patterns so you can get unstuck.

See Your Pattern

The core of the Lagging Transparency pattern that we identified in our research is that organizations value reactive transparency more than they value proactive transparency, which was rooted in a competing commitment: the commitment to sharing information is neutralized by a commitment to controlling information. Now think about where this pattern is causing friction inside your organization:

- Is a lack of strategic clarity causing people to head off in the wrong direction too frequently?
- Are data inaccessible because different departments keep them locked down?
- Is the rumor mill hurting morale because people invent stories about what the senior level is thinking?
- Are people missing opportunities because others don't think they need to know the information?

Keep asking questions like this until you've identified the most prominent examples of culture friction. That will be your guide for determining what needs to change to improve your culture.

Get Unstuck

Chapter 6 provides the playbook model for culture change, but take note of some of the plays that Pinion ran in order to defeat the lagging transparency pattern:

- Building out a robust intranet as part of their transparency architecture [technology]
- Sharing KPIs at both organizational and individual levels with everyone [process, technology]
- Doubling down on professional development [talent/HR]

And that's just the start. Here are some plays other organizations have used to address this pattern.

- **Switch from Performance Reports to 360 Reviews.** HR will create a process to allow for structured, anonymous feedback regarding management performance. [talent/HR]
- **New Employee Orientation.** Improve the new employee orientation/onboarding process. Include a consistent approach to orienting new staff, laying the foundation for a shared understanding of learning goals that support our Core Competencies. [talent/HR]
- **CEO Video Updates.** Short weekly or monthly video messages from the CEO that the entire company can view to share strategic updates and initiatives. They can be posted to the intranet and promoted in the newsletter. [process]
- **VP of Corporate Communications & Transparency.** Hire a senior-level internal communications professional whose responsibility is to drive transparency in the company. [structure/design]
- **KPIs.** Determine and prominently display clearly defined KPIs, both organization-wide and for specific product lines. [process]

Can you think of other culture plays that would work for you? Go to culturechangemadeeasybook.com where you'll find a place to browse more plays and submit your own ideas and experiments.

CHAPTER 4

Heavy Agility

BOTTOM LINE

Organizations that suffer from Heavy Agility value forward action more than they value effective action.

- We excel at creating cultures that take action, move quickly, and embrace change as a fact of life in the workplace. People can generally make decisions, even if they are not in charge.
- We struggle, however, with continuously making sure that our actions are effective and efficient. We're always pushing forward and don't take the time to fix things that are broken and to stop things that are no longer providing value. We focus too much on who owns things, rather than who is best to get it done.
- The competing commitment that drives this pattern includes a strong commitment to adaptability and speed that is neutralized by a commitment to creation and novelty. These organizations genuinely want

to be agile but by always moving to what's new they reduce their capacity to be nimble, and as a result, they miss opportunities, frustrate their employees, and leave money on the table.

The problem with this Culture Pattern is that it creates opportunity gaps that result in lost potential.

- We tolerate processes that don't work well (and everyone knows it), reducing morale and leading to higher turnover.
- We push hard to change and move fast, but end up slower than expected, missing opportunities to create value.

Solutions to this problem include a deeper focus on learning, data, and co-creation.

- Our case study organization created a culture that prioritizes learning, evaluating priorities every three months.
- They also are disciplined about their use of data, applying it to strategic decisions and operational issues, like job descriptions.
- They are committed to co-creating the business with their customers, letting new developments emerge based on customer input.

How you can solve it:

- See your pattern: identify the specific areas where culture friction is messing with success, like wasted effort as decisions get made and then un-made, or missed opportunities because people are spread too thin.
- Get unstuck: run culture plays like after-action reviews and processes for sunsetting projects.

Did the Pandemic Make Us Agile?

Before the pandemic, most managers would have told you that working from home is a bad idea. They had a slew of arguments:

- People will use it to avoid paying for child care and will take care of their kids most of the day.
- We won't be able to hold people accountable if they end up doing laundry instead of working.
- People working from home will not be "reachable" when something important comes up.
- In short, if I can't see you or walk into your office, then you won't do your work and it won't be effective.

That is why, as of late 2019, 60% of workers were in the office full-time, and only 8% were working fully remotely. The rest were working a "hybrid" schedule—something with which we are all familiar now—but back then it was more limited. It was typically reserved for more senior leaders, and it happened more frequently in the form of the occasional day here and there, compared to multiple days per week as we see now.

Then in March 2020, the coronavirus pandemic put us into lockdown. The 8% working fully remote jumped to 70%—in a matter of a few days. And those 70% stayed fully remote for quite some time. There was a lot of intention to go "back to the office" in the fall of 2021 and then again around the new year in 2022, but the resurging delta and omicron variants of the virus delayed those plans. But over that year, a lot of people started working at the office more. By the end of the year, the number working fully remotely was down to 26%, and the largest percentage belonged to people on a hybrid schedule (53%).[1]

That's a staggering change. The number of fully remote employees

1 Vox Media. (December 9, 2022). Share of workers working onsite versus hybrid or remote in the United States from 2019 to 4th quarter 2022 [Graph]. In Statista. Accessed August 12, 2023, from https://www.statista.com/statistics/1356325/hybrid-vs-remote-work-us/

is up by 300% and we only have 21% on location full-time (and a lot of those are not in office environments). And guess what happened:

- The work got done.
- Accountability didn't disappear.
- People were reachable.

To be clear, there is value in doing work together in person, and some activities are particularly less effective when you try to do them remotely, but all of the pre-pandemic predictions about how horrible working from home would be didn't really pan out. The fact is, we may not be perfect at it, but we figured out how to make remote work, work.

That sounds remarkably agile, doesn't it? Nearly all of us had to learn a new way of working, using new technologies, all while figuring out how to deliver our products and services to customers in sometimes radically new ways. Even as things became more "normal" in 2023, the pace of change did not seem to subside. Canadian Prime Minister Justin Trudeau seemed to be preparing us for this moment back in 2018 at the World Economic Forum when he said, "The pace of change has never been this fast, yet it will never be this slow again."[2]

We will be the first to admit that we did not have "organizations will become incredibly agile in the face of a global pandemic" on our bingo cards at the end of 2019. **Of all the eight Culture Markers we measure in our assessment, Agility scores as the least present in cultures.** In fact, it makes you wonder—given our demonstrated ability to handle that much change in a short amount of time, do we even need a chapter on agility in a book about culture change anymore?

Yes, we do.

---

2 https://www.youtube.com/watch?v=fTl1YNTNb0g Accessed August 2023.

The Problem: Heavy Agility

Why? Because agility does not simply mean change. Aaron de Smet, a Principal at McKinsey, defines agility in the organizational context as "the ability of an organization to renew itself, adapt, change quickly, and succeed in a rapidly changing, ambiguous, turbulent environment."[3] So yes, agility means changing quickly, but it's more than that. It requires *renewal,* implying that we have achieved some new level of energy so we can start fresh. It requires *adaptation* so that the new state is now considered normal. The adaptation must make you more *successful,* implying that the change was strategically designed to meet a new challenge, not just a stopgap measure to get you through the day temporarily.

We would argue that organizations succeeded at changing rapidly through the pandemic, but they have not been agile. The compelling evidence in favor of that argument is burnout.

According to a report from the American Psychological Association in 2021,

> Nearly 3 in 5 employees reported negative impacts of work-related stress, including lack of interest, motivation, or energy (26%) and lack of effort at work (19%). Meanwhile, 36% reported cognitive weariness, 32% reported emotional exhaustion, and an astounding 44% reported physical fatigue—a 38% increase since 2019.[4]

We changed like crazy, but now we're exhausted because change and agility are not the same thing. **The pandemic proved that just about any organization can change, but it is not evidence of any kind of growth in organizations' ability to be truly agile.** In fact, that exhaustion

3   https://www.mckinsey.com/capabilities/people-and-organizational-performance/
    our-insights/the-keys-to-organizational-agility Accessed August 2023.
4   https://www.apa.org/monitor/2022/01/special-burnout-stress Accessed August 2023.

we're feeling is directly connected to the Culture Pattern that many organizations experience, called Heavy Agility.

While most cultures do embrace change at a high level and work diligently to move quickly while still maintaining quality, they have not built up the capacity to fix things that are broken and stop things that are no longer providing value. They do the change, but they fail to truly adapt and renew themselves, and chronic inefficiency, waste, and missed opportunities are the result.

Here is how this Culture Pattern often shows up:

- Competitors beat you to the punch and steal market share because you couldn't respond to a shift in customer demand fast enough.
- Despite successful products and services, turnover is high due to frustration with all the inefficiencies.
- New things get added, but nothing gets taken off anyone's plate and the resulting burnout hurts quality.
- Everyone takes criticism personally and nobody will admit that something's broken or is no longer needed, so we push through with inadequate processes.

This is what Heavy Agility looks like in the real world. We aren't good at fixing things and stopping things, so it's like we're running a race with weights tied around our ankles. We manage to cross the finish line and might even improve our times compared to the year before, but we're falling well short of our potential, and the exhaustion from the extra effort takes its toll on our morale. Why? Because we overemphasize moving forward and underemphasize effectiveness and efficiency.

What is Heavy Agility?

Organizations with the Heavy Agility Culture Pattern value forward action more than they value effective action.

In other words, they are making great efforts to maintain speed without losing quality, and they embrace change at a high level, yet there is not enough attention put toward fixing things that are broken or stopping activities that no longer add value.

The competing commitment behind this pattern rests on a solid commitment to adaptability and speed that is neutralized by a commitment to novelty and creation. Employees are drawn to creating new things and pay less attention to fixing or stopping things that already exist. In that sense, they are achieving agility without having shed some of the weight that was slowing them down to begin with, hence the term "Heavy Agility." These cultures do move quickly, but they still haven't figured out how to manage hierarchy in a way that unleashes real agility, and their inability to consistently fix things or stop things when needed is holding them back.

The aggregate data from our culture assessment reveals the pattern clearly. Employees across the board report that things like "managing change" and "quality management" were more present in the culture, but those are about moving forward. But the questions that focused on making sure the forward movement is effective ("efficiency" and "changing directions") were not as present. As a result, they are experiencing culture friction and drag.

How Heavy Agility Shows Up: Opportunity Gaps

Although organizations put in a lot of effort to bring about change, they often fall short of their full potential due to their inability to stop or fix things when required. This creates what we call opportunity gaps. As a result of our lack of agility, we miss opportunities for growth and improvement. These gaps can be tricky to identify, as the outcome may still be acceptable, even though it is not reaching its full potential. We get comfortable doing things the way we've always done them, and we tolerate inefficiencies because we feel our results are adequate.

Interestingly, the business world has had access to a tool for eliminating these opportunity gaps for decades: Lean Six Sigma. Six Sigma was pioneered by companies like Motorola and General Electric in the 1980s and 1990s, and it was a process for reducing defects in manufacturing. Lean manufacturing has its roots in the "Toyota way" but was further developed in the 2000s as a component of Six Sigma. Where Six Sigma focuses on reducing defects, lean focuses on eliminating waste, so they are focused squarely on the effective action component of Heavy Agility: they are about fixing things and stopping things. There are countless stories of large manufacturing organizations that recorded millions of dollars in cost savings and additional profits that they could tie directly to the quality improvement achieved by using Lean Six Sigma methods to fix things and stop things.

But you don't have to be a large manufacturing company to apply the methods. Marie Kondo's famous art of decluttering, for example, has been described as an example of Lean Six Sigma.[5] We even found an example in the world of fine dining.

Sandro Nardone is a high-end chef in Orange County, California. He was born into a family of chefs in Italy, and when he started his restaurant in America, he wanted to bring over his family's recipe for a seafood dish called *aqua pazza*. This dish involves cooking a whole fish in water and aromatics (*aqua pazza* in Italian literally means "crazy water"), and once it's done, the fish is fileted and then served in the broth used to cook the fish. But here's the challenge: in a large American restaurant, you don't have time to filet every fish individually before it's served.

Nardone had an opportunity gap. In other words, the solution that his family had developed in Italy worked just fine in that context, but in a new context, the process would not be successful. It needed to be fixed. So he applied Six Sigma. He identified the element of the process that was producing the defect and fixed it. In this case, he changed the process to prepare the broth ahead of time, and then cook the previously fileted fish in the broth. The dish became a success, winning a local award.[6]

5   "Marie Kondo And The Art Of Lean," *Lean & Six Sigma Review,* May 2020, Volume 19, Issue 3, pp. 10-17.
6   https://bellobysandronardone.com/aqua-pazza-as-an-example-of-six-sigma/ Accessed August 2023.

If a high-end chef can apply Six Sigma to the artistry of fine dining, why can't a financial planning organization improve its employee onboarding process? Why can't a nonprofit get its database to provide effective reports in a timely manner? Why can't a doctor's office improve its customer service? The problem is Heavy Agility and it creates opportunity gaps like these all the time.

The employee onboarding example is one of the most glaring opportunity gaps in the business world. According to a 2019 Gallup study, only 1 out of 8 employees think their organization does a great job at employee onboarding. If you Google "why can't we fix employee onboarding" you will find a seemingly endless list of articles giving you the 4, 5, 7, or 10 ways your onboarding process is broken and how to fix them. It's as if the internet has already done some Lean Six Sigma work for you to identify the waste and defects.

Yet even with good answers out there, very few organizations take action to fix this broken process. Let's say you have a position that is tough to fill. The person previously in the position went back to school, so several months go by before you can find a new person. That means other staff have been covering those functions, in addition to their regular jobs, and stress is high. Once that new person arrives, you will want them to get to work as soon as possible, thus your onboarding process ends up looking something like this:
- Lunch out with the team,
- Lots of manuals and policies to read,
- A walk around the office to meet key people in other departments,
- Now get to work.

Unfortunately, less than a year later, your new employee leaves. In the exit interview, they talk about feeling like they weren't set up for success in the role. They didn't understand how the different parts of the organization were supposed to work together, they couldn't see the connection between their work and organizational strategy, and they weren't clear on their career path opportunities at this organization—all of which could have been addressed by a good onboarding process.

Even when we see that, of course, we fail to change the process, because now we're stressed out about having to fill that position again. We tolerate our own ineffectiveness, which is a hallmark of the Heavy Agility Culture Pattern. If you want to fix that, then you must understand the inner workings of the pattern itself.

Breaking the Pattern Down: Forward Action v. Effective Action

Like the other Culture Patterns, organizations excel in one part of the pattern, but struggle with the other. **For agility, most organizations excel at forward action but struggle with effective action.**

Where We Excel: Forward Action

In traditional management, change was something that took a long time, was carefully controlled, and was a significant disruption to operations. Think about it in the context of a manufacturing facility—to make a change to the assembly line would require a complete shutdown of operations for an extended period of time. There wasn't a particular desire for speed. For those of you who are old enough to remember the classic "chocolate factory" episode of *I Love Lucy*,[7] increasing speed in a manufacturing context by definition meant a decrease in quality, so it was rarely an objective.

Today, most organizations have moved away from that approach, though of all the Culture Markers we measure, Agility is the most traditional. In our aggregate culture assessment data, Agility scores 3.52 out of 5, which is well below the overall average of 3.69. The next closest would be Technologies and Transparency, each at 3.60, and Culture Markers like Inclusion and Collaboration are a full three-tenths higher. That said, Agility follows the same pattern as all of the Culture Markers, with three of the specific

---

7 You can see the clip here: https://www.youtube.com/watch?v=AnHiAWlrYQc

Building Blocks showing up as more futurist than the rest:
- Quality management
- Managing change
- Decision making and problem solving

Those three combined averaged 3.66, which is above the score for Agility as a whole, though still below the overall average. These Building Blocks represent the foundation for an organization that values agility. Most organizations believe that they do fairly well at moving quickly while still maintaining quality, and they also embrace change, at least at a high level. It would be difficult to even survive in today's environment if there weren't at least some commitment to those two principles. They also, for the most part, want people to be able to make decisions, even if they're not in charge. These approaches help organizations move forward.

If you do forward action well in your culture, you will have created an environment where quality matters and is measured consistently, and, more importantly, if the environment requires you to pick up the pace of your work, the quality won't suffer. When one of your customers places an unusually large order, you should be able to reorganize people's work in a way that meets the demand and doesn't miss the deadline.

Change, for the most part, is accepted as a normal part of doing business and is not feared or avoided. **Organizations that do forward action well actually like change, and they are looking for opportunities to make changes rather than grumbling about the need to adapt.** When feedback comes in that a product or service is no longer meeting the customer's needs as well, there is excitement in the opportunity to change your offering and wow the customer.

And while hierarchy obviously still counts in your culture, **you also recognize that speed sometimes requires people who are not "in charge" to be able to make decisions.** An over-reliance on hierarchy can slow things down, so people in your organization have learned how to responsibly move outside of prescribed authority lines at times, when it will move the organization forward.

Cultures like that have a clear commitment to moving forward and accessing speed when necessary. They embrace change at a high level. But these commit-ments do not address the work it takes to make sure that all your forward action is truly effective, as we will illustrate below.

Where We Struggle: Effective Action

In Chapter 3 on Lagging Transparency, we gave several examples of how the software company Menlo Innovation put transparency into practice. Menlo also demonstrates what it takes to be agile, because they have built into their processes several interesting components that ensure their actions are effective.

First, they use a coding process called paired programming, where two developers write code together using one computer. While one person is typing code, the other is reading the code and offering real-time feedback. While it may seem to be an inefficient use of resources, it turns out it makes them faster and produces higher quality software, because most of the bugs in the code are caught earlier on in the process.

They also have a process where the customers who are paying for the custom software come into their offices once every week to review the progress and see any components that are finished enough to present. Again, most organizations would shy away from showing unfinished work to paying customers, but by getting their reactions earlier on, they are able to make adjustments more quickly and effectively. So not only are they moving quickly with quality, they are continuously evaluating the quality of their decisions and they can fix things—and even get rid of components of the software—without extra or wasted effort.

That disciplined commitment to effective action is quite rare in organiza-tions today. **We see many organizations committed to the concept of agility, but most of them are unable to do the basic blocking and tackling that true agility requires.** In this case, the piece of traditional management that organizations are unwilling to give up is its linear nature. In traditional management, all processes have a beginning, a middle, and an end. Once you started something, you followed it through to its designed conclusion. Even if it's not working out the way you hoped, you would often have to finish the entire linear process before you could do some redesigning and launch it again. Similarly, in organizations with the Heavy Agility Culture Pattern, when something is in progress, there is typically little opportunity for circling back to make changes, even if you realize something isn't quite right.

Many organizations today may not realize it, but they are sticking with the traditional approach. **Even though we know that we should fix things that are broken and stop things that are no longer providing value, we don't do it as much as we should.** We see this in the three Culture Building Blocks within agility that have low scores in our aggregate data set:

- Assignment of responsibility
- Efficiency
- Changing directions

These three Blocks combined averaged only 3.38, the lowest score of any of the 16 pattern components. Efficiency and Changing Directions were particularly traditional, individually ranking 58 and 63 out of 64. These elements are simply not very present in most cultures today.

All three of these Culture Building Blocks are about improving effectiveness. The *assignment of responsibility* Block is about sharing work based on who is in the best position to get it done, rather than who "owns" it. **When you skew towards ownership, you are feeding the commitment to novelty and creation, because you are valuing people's ability to create and shape their own programs, rather than focusing on what would make the program more effective.** Organizations that score higher on this Block have employees that see the bigger picture around value creation and don't tie it to their egos.

The *efficiency* Block is about stopping things. When a program or process is no longer providing the value it once was, logic dictates that it should be stopped. As we mentioned, however, the changing direction block is 63rd out of 64 Blocks, which means most organizations are not very good at stopping things. As with the changing directions Block (see below), **we end up tolerating activity that is not producing value, which reduces our effectiveness.** Organizations that are better in this area often have formal program evaluation processes to ensure that only the most successful activities are continued.

The *changing directions* Block is about fixing things. The rating statement in our assessment is "if a process or procedure is not working, we can correct it with ease." The very low scores organizations provide indicate that fixing things that are broken is not particularly easy. **That means they are tolerating inefficiency or doing end-runs around broken procedures.** The organizations that score higher in this area tend to be more disciplined in their project management, allocating time and resources to fix what's broken earlier on.

How to Fix Heavy Agility

The trick to fixing the Heavy Agility pattern is learning how to get out of your own way. **We often try to improve agility by pushing harder or running faster, but there is usually a better ROI for putting effort into removing obstacles and smoothing the path.** This shift in orientation requires some interesting changes to your culture.

Matchbox Virtual Media is a virtual event company with an interesting story that illustrates what it takes to overcome the Heavy Agility pattern. Their story includes both rapid growth and rapid contraction, all fueled by the pandemic. Launched in 2019, they were in the virtual event space even before the pandemic hit. It's almost hard to remember the Before Times, but prior to the pandemic, virtual events were already a thing. People did, in fact, use tools like Zoom and Webex for interactive online meetings of all sizes. For the larger ones, like virtual conferences, Matchbox was a company you could hire to run the whole show for you.

So when the pandemic hit, Matchbox was suddenly and very much in demand. "From year one to year two, our revenue grew twenty-fold, and we went from a team of five to a team of fifty in eight months," said Arianna Rehak, Matchbox's CEO. But almost as quickly as demand rose, a year later it started to flatten out. Meeting in person was once again an option, and while virtual meetings did not disappear entirely, the demand fell to a point where Matchbox realized that the business it had built during the Pandemic could no longer exist.

That was a tough time for Matchbox, and they had to lay off a large number of employees, to the point where they thought they might just go under. As Rehak reflected,

> I remember at that time, one of the founders said, in desperation, "We need to take whatever business we can to survive." And I said to him, if we're in that place, there's no reason for us to exist. Why not go off and do other things in the world?

Instead of going under, they pivoted. They moved away from being purely a service company that would run virtual events, and they built a virtual platform designed to automate the parts of the process that proved to be the most time-consuming for both their team and their clients. They have a smaller core team now, bolstered with contractor support, but they are back on a growth trajectory. In 2023 they validated their new direction by forming a joint venture with the Endocrine Society, a medical nonprofit whose investment is accelerating their build-out and helping them automate processes specific to serving more medical, healthcare, and scientific associations.

They showed they were capable of true agility—not just rapid change. They shifted and morphed in ways that were generative, delivering renewal to the organization, not just surviving the stress of change. There were three aspects of their culture that helped them achieve this kind of agility:

- Learning
- Data
- Co-creation

Build a Learning Culture

Peter Senge published his best-seller, *The Fifth Discipline*, more than thirty years ago, the subtitle of which is "The Art and Practice of the Learning Organization," so learning is not a new concept in organizations. We also wrote about it more than ten years ago in *Humanize*. Learning was the hallmark of the culture of what we described as a "courageous" organization:

> [Courageous organizations] spend more effort to develop
> a deeper sense of what is and an understanding of how
> the organization's behavior impacts the broader system.
> They are comfortable letting their learning actually change
> the organization, even the organization's basic identity.[8]

That sounds a lot like Matchbox, doesn't it? They have been, in fact, courageous in the way they reinvented their organization, and they explicitly recognize the role and importance of learning as part of that process.

One of the most important areas to inject learning into your culture is in the development and implementation of strategy. We argued ten years ago in *Humanize* that strategic planning is inherently defective. Strategic planning, as it has been traditionally practiced, is about making decisions about where to focus and allocate resources, resulting in a fairly detailed and linear three-year plan. While there's nothing wrong with making strategic bets that might take three years to pay off, strategic planning ruins things by writing up a sequential plan, because that takes learning out of the picture.

We all know that the operating environment will change drastically over a three-year period, so why are we wasting time mapping out a three-year plan? Matchbox would agree.

> We're going through a strategic planning exercise right
> now, and I told the person facilitating, "I don't know
> how far out we should be planning, because I don't want
> to lose sight of learning from the market and experiences
> if we, on this day, decide these are the goals that we're going
> to pursue.

They are developing more of a "strategic framework" that will guide decision-making, rather than a detailed plan, and learning is integrated into it. With their new focus on building a self-service platform that is automating the most tedious processes in virtual events, they are now in a phase

---

8   Notter and Grant, Humanize (2012), p. 223.

of working to deeply understand the on-the-ground realities of the customers they are serving. A strategic framework is much better suited for their purposes, recognizing that plans must sometimes shift with new information.

In his book, *Scaling Up*, Verne Harnish presents an approach to strategy that integrates learning as well. Harnish created the Entrepreneurs' Organization and has used his approach to help entrepreneurs grow their businesses, but the approach is applicable to businesses of any size. At the heart of his approach is what he calls a "one-page strategic plan."[9]

It's a single document (that, to be honest, is almost always a bit longer than one page) that creates a clear strategic line-of-sight, from long-term vision down to priorities and metrics that look only 90 days out. It does include goals that cover a three-year time horizon, but it does not include any plans at all for what is going to happen in years two or three, as traditional strategic plans do. Even the one-year objectives are not fully fleshed out, because the real planning activities are done quarterly.

Every quarter, you identify 3-5 priorities. Harnish calls these "rocks," alluding to the metaphor of filling a container with big rocks, smaller rocks, pebbles, and sand—if you want them to fit, then you must put the big rocks in first to allow the smaller ones to fill the gaps. Your quarterly rocks are the highest priority items that must be accomplished over the next three months, based on the strategic model you've built for your longer-term success.

We want to emphasize the word "model" in that last sentence. **Instead of building a linear three-year plan, you build a model of what it will take to reach those three-year objectives.** That can still involve some projecting out of potential strategic moves or investments down the road, but a model has one key advantage over a plan: all models are wrong.

George Box was a British statistician who gained notoriety for his pithy quote, "all models are wrong, but some are useful."[10] A model, by definition, is not the thing that it is modeling. We do not get inside a model airplane

9   Verne Harnish, *Scaling Up: How a Few Companies Make It…and Why the Rest Don't* (Gazelles, 2014).

10 https://en.wikipedia.org/wiki/All_models_are_wrong Accessed September 2023.

and fly to Los Angeles in it. In that sense, you don't need or want a model to be 100% "right." But you do want it to be useful. That same model airplane could prove to be very useful if it's something your young child can play with on the flight to LA.

Box was referring to mathematical models which are not true in every single circumstance, but do provide useful approximations that can be applied in real situations. The same is true for strategic models. Your model for what will get you to your three-year targets is not going to be perfect, but it can serve as a useful guide for making decisions about what to do in the next three months.

And what you do in the next three months can end up improving your model. This is where learning comes in, which then enables strategic agility. By setting three-month objectives, you provide continuous opportunities for learning. This is one reason why Harnish insists on writing the quarterly rocks as binary outcomes—you either hit the objective, or you don't. "Improve the quality of the output from the manufacturing operation" is too vague, but "Achieve a defect rate of less than 10 parts per 1,000 by the end of the quarter" is fine. It's binary. You'll either hit that mark or you won't.

That sharpens your ability to learn from it. If you don't hit the mark, you explore why. If you do hit the mark, you can explore why your target might have been too conservative. Everything we achieve or don't achieve is an opportunity for learning. And when you compound that learning every three months, it enables you to make significant strategic shifts much earlier in the process.

Despite Matchbox's willingness to adapt when needed, they did have a moment in their brief history where they felt like they weren't agile enough— during the decline in their business, once their clients went back to in-person meetings. The data were pretty clear, indicating a need to cut staff and downsize, but the leadership found itself shifting to a more qualitative approach to the decision-making. As Kristov Martens, Chief Business Officer, put it,

> We were not agile on the descent, and that hurt us. We were very proud of the team and the culture we built. And it was hard for us to fathom sacrificing even

one or two team members when we realized we couldn't support the salaries or didn't have the business coming in. In reality, we needed to cut deeply, and take a step back as a business and come back at the market again from a new direction.

This connects back to Adam Grant's concept of confident humility that we mentioned in the previous chapter. Learning requires you to have only a loose grip on the solutions you've chosen, where you're humble enough to know that they could be wrong. Holding on too tightly, in this case, driven by the pride associated with creating something good, can reduce your agility.

Rigorous Data

The section above on Verne Harnish's quarterly rocks also illustrates the next factor inside Matchbox's culture that enabled agility, and that is what Rehak described as being "unforgivingly rigorous around data." Once again, in *Humanize,* we pointed to the importance of data in supporting better learning conversations inside organizations:

> Human organizations have a fondness for data, and the really good ones flat out love data. They love to analyze it and slice it and dice it in the learning process to make better decisions. They get data from many different sources, at different times, with an almost insatiable curiosity.[11]

Matchbox also has that insatiable curiosity. When they graduated out of the beta version of their platform, they "obsessively" watched the initial users. As Rehak explains,

> We didn't want to have preconceived notions around how the tool was going to be used; we wanted the data to guide us. That principle is also true in the digital products

---

11   Notter and Grant, *Humanize* (2012), p. 225.

that we're helping clients create, because we're using the data of what's actually happening to iterate. In both of those scenarios, the most powerful people in the process were ones that came at things without any preconceived notions of what they were looking at.

This connects to the "ladder of inference" model that we described in Chapter 2 on Awkward Collaboration. It's a model for understanding how humans observe things in the world, draw conclusions about them, and then take actions based on those conclusions. The very bottom of the ladder is "data," or observable experiences. Technically, this represents all of objective reality, but as humans, it is impossible to take in all of reality (from every perspective), so our first step up the ladder is to "select" some of the data based on our experiences.

In other words, what we all know to be true in this world is actually based on observing a fairly small sliver of reality. And to make that sliver even smaller, we're really only operating on the observable experiences that we can remember. The truth is, we recall only a small percentage of what we experience every day.

The next step in making sense of things is to add our own personal meaning to the pieces of data that we remember. This happens automatically, without even thinking about it, and the meaning that we add is based on our own personal history. This is where things get a bit messy. We're observing something today, but we instantly add meaning based on experiences that we had in the past, which might not be relevant. To further complicate matters, the data we have is never enough to see the whole picture, so we also end up making assumptions to fill in the gaps. Only after climbing up all those rungs of the ladder of inference do we draw conclusions.

There is nothing wrong this process—it's just the way our brains work, but this is where the "pre-conceived notions" to which Rehak was referring develop, and they can steer you down the wrong path. You could be watching a customer who fails to use one of the platform's features, and your brain could run quickly up the ladder to conclude the language in the menu items is not clear (because that's what you had experienced in another context), when, in fact, the user simply sees no value in that feature.

Matchbox actually worked with a data scientist to help them break that bad habit.

> I remember that we had a data scientist we were work-
> ing with over the COVID period, and frequently I would
> say something, and then she would very tactfully respond,
> "That's an assumption. Do we actually know that's the case?"
> Of course, we didn't know that's the case, so she'd ask,
> "What do the data say?"

Using user data to improve software products is a fairly established practice, but Matchbox doesn't only apply its rigorous focus on data in that context. They recently began a pilot of a four-day work week, a concept that has been growing in popularity since the pandemic. According to the Wall Street Journal, one long-term study cites positive results of such experiments, resulting in less burnout and lower turnover without a loss in productivity.[12] Those results are exactly what Matchbox is focused on with their pilot, according to Chief Business officer:

> I think that's a big shift in our culture to move to that
> model. So we need to be able to track productivity. Is this
> improving employee well-being? Is this reducing turnover?
> Is this not affecting our interactions with clients? These
> are all questions we're going to be asking ourselves while
> we do the pilot, so this is what we want to be tracking.

They even applied data to help improve employee engagement for one of their newer employees, named Nina. She came to the CEO with an "I love this company, but I'm hating my day-to-day job right now" moment. She found herself doing a lot of manual and repetitive tasks that weren't terribly fulfilling. So the Matchbox team banded together to start working with

12 https://www.wsj.com/articles/the-four-day-workweek-gets-shorter-with-practice-
companies-find-edc9eb2f Accessed September 2023.

her on a data-driven process to solve the problem.

They started by having her track her time rigorously for two weeks and then enter it all into a spreadsheet, including the tasks she completed and how long each task took. She then rated her enjoyment of each activity on a scale of -3 to +3. As they examined the data, they saw that nearly all of the tasks with low ratings (-3 or -2) were manual tasks that could be automated. Similarly, the things that she loved doing turned out to be activities that were of the highest value to the organization and the clients, yet she didn't have time to do as many of those things because of all the manual tasks. So they got to work automating things, allowing them to free up close to 30% of her time, which could then be spent on higher-value work.

This exercise had an additional benefit to the company's mission, recognizing that a lot of the work this team member was doing fell into the category of "managed services," which meant that a lot of their clients could be feeling a similar lack of engagement. As Rehak shared,

> We called it Operation: Automating Nina. Nina became our litmus test. If we could make her work more fulfilling by automating the tedious processes, it meant we were doing the same for the current and future users of our self-service platform.

There is one potential downside to a focus on data as it relates to agility, and that is analysis paralysis. **If you obsess over the data, it is unlikely that your culture will be successful in fixing things and stopping things, which are two keys to agility.** In *The Lean Startup,* Eric Ries suggests creating "minimum viable products" (MVPs) as an antidote to this problem. Instead of doing endless focus groups with customers to find out exactly what they want so you can build the perfect product, get something—even if it's imperfect—into the customers' hands, so they can provide feedback on something tangible, rather than a hypothetical issue.

It's still about creating new products or services based on data, but it intentionally limits the amount of data to avoid paralysis. The idea of an MVP also shortens the timeframe of data collection so that the system is always reintegrating lessons from the data collection back into the next version. This is why our computer software is being continuously updated these days. Apps are never perfect out of the gate—they are tested on real users and improved over time (or sunsetted).

Applying the concepts in Verne Harnish's quarterly planning system is another way to avoid analysis paralysis. As we mentioned above in the section on strategy, the system is based on creating a new model every quarter and then learning from what actually happened to help you build a more effective model for the next quarter.

Matchbox now applies a similar approach to its sales and marketing activities. They had previously attempted to do a rigorous analysis of historical sales data in order to map out their activity, but realized that the learning from that data—which was during COVID—was no longer applicable because that period was such an anomaly. Instead, they build a continuously evolving model. It's a set of sales/marketing hypotheses that inform their pricing model, sales approach, and customer success philosophy. As Rehak explains,

> We take this time to step back and look at them at a high level, but on a day-to-day basis we are committed to breaking our rules sometimes due to the possibility that an edge case may not actually be an edge case. Over time we will start to converge in such a way that breaking rules may not be worth it (such as taking on pilot projects that are outside of our core focus) but for now allowing in some unusual data points is helping us formulate the picture of what our steady state will one day look like.

Co-Creation with Customers and Employees

The third way that Matchbox overcame the Heavy Agility Culture Pattern was by co-creating things with both customers and employees. Co-creation as a management concept has been around for more than 20 years. CK Prahalad and Venkat Ramaswamy coined the term in a *Harvard Business Review* article in 2000, though the concept had been developed in Europe and the U.S. as far back as the 1980s.[13] The initial focus of the concept was on the idea of collaborating with customers in the creation of new products, which fed into the trend of open innovation that was emerging at the time (and, a bit later, the internet-fueled concept of crowdsourcing).

Ultimately, co-creation is a part of design thinking and is sometimes referred to as user-centric design. Eventually, the focus spread to encompass employees as well as users/customers, which we explored in *When Millennials Take Over* as a part of our coverage of the "digital mindset." The digital age has allowed companies to provide much more user-centric service, and we gave the example of how the casino company, Ceasar's Entertainment, used customer data to provide "high roller" services to the vast middle of their market[14]. We mentioned in the previous chapter that the non-profit ASSH applies this to employees by customizing the job descriptions of every employee, every year, based on their unique career trajectories. That's co-creation.

Co-creating is one of Matchbox's four core values, which they apply equally to both customers and employees. As VP of Marketing Michelle Brien explains, the customer is always put at the center of the journey:

> One of the things that I love is the idea of really putting the customer at the center of the whole journey. We realigned our sales, marketing, and customer success teams to make sure that the customers have that really great experience, from the beginning right on through.

To be clear, **co-creating with customers is different from merely paying attention to customers or caring about customer experience.** Everyone cares about customers. In our data, "customer influence" is one of the highest scoring questions at 4.18, ranking 5th out of the 64 Building Blocks

---

13   https://medium.com/future-work-design/a-brief-history-of-co-creation-2e4d615189e8 Accessed September 2023.

14   Notter and Grant, *Millennials* (2015), pp. 38-39.

we measure. It doesn't really vary by industry or the size of the organization. We all focus on customers (members, donors, clients, stakeholders, etc.).

Customer focus, however, doesn't seem to generate the interest and energy that Brien expressed above when she talked about putting customers at the center of the journey. We measure correlation with each of the Building Blocks in our data set with the one question that is more focused on employee engagement (the "would you recommend someone to work here" question). Of all of the questions, the customer influence question has the lowest correlation with engagement (+0.26, which is considered a weak correlation).

Matchbox goes way beyond mere customer focus and has intentionally built deeper co-creation into their culture. Everyone they hire buys in to the approach. According to Paolo Melgarejo, the Chief Technology Officer,

> Everyone on the team is like that. They cater to the clients and actually listen. We don't even call them clients; they're almost like friends or colleagues, or partners even. That's the type of culture that Matchbox cultivates. So we're actively always listening and it's baked into our process from beginning to end.

Co-creation is so central to what they do, that they've also extended it to how they work with each other as employees. If they run into a sticky problem on a project, they quickly create a Google Doc and list the key questions they have about that problem. There's a column in the document for anyone to put in answers to those questions, and there's another column labeled "yes, and" where people can respond to the responses. It's all done asynchronously, and there's really no way to let hierarchy or experience level have undue influence in the process. They are co-creating together.

They are also demonstrating clearly the impact co-creating has on agility. Remember, the Heavy Agility pattern has organizations valuing forward action more than effective action. They move quickly, but they don't take time to stop things and fix things. Co-creation engages everyone in the system in figuring out what needs to be fixed or stopped. There was a similar dynamic in the way Menlo Innovations would bring their client into their office on a weekly basis to review the progress of their software design project.

Changing directions and pivoting when needed thus becomes easy, and because everyone was involved in the process, there is much less resistance. Co-creating is often viewed as a luxury, because it means adding steps to the process, and it's true, that can take more time, but the time you spend on co-creation is usually made up by the time you save by making shifts before it's too late.

Co-creation also requires a certain level of trust and the ability to let go of control. This is part of what enables the behaviors that overcome the Heavy Agility pattern, because both trust and letting go of control unlock speed. When you let go of control, and give it over to customers and co-workers, you make the right changes faster, enabling you to fix things and stop things sooner. A foundation of trust enables you to take the right leaps—including firing your biggest client.

Remember that Matchbox made some big shifts in its short history. Their initial growth was in producing virtual events, but as they switched to developing a software solution, one of their biggest clients was still paying them to produce some virtual events. CEO Rehak reflected on the tough decision that faced the team:

> The work we were doing for them was very different from where we were going. The money that's coming in is paying for our employees, which is great, but those employees are spending time doing something that isn't what our business is. So I had to take a leap of faith and cut off that contract.

The decision has paid off for them, and it's a good reflection of the "effective action" part of this Culture Pattern. When they are faced with a new situation, they're not paralyzed. As Nina Blake (of Operation Automating Nina fame), Customer Success Manager, said:

> When we have a new client who's looking for a different type of experience that we've never encountered, in the past, it would have caused kind of a weird halt—we've never encountered this... Whereas now it's more, okay this makes sense.

How You Can Fix This Culture Pattern

A focus on building a learning culture, rigorous attention to data, and co-creation with customers and employees can help you overcome the pattern of Heavy Agility, but they are not the only ways. Here is how to start seeing your patterns so you can get unstuck.

See Your Pattern

The core of the Heavy Agility pattern that we identified in our research is that organizations value forward action more than they value effective action, which was rooted in a competing commitment: the commitment to adaptability and speed is neutralized by a commitment to newness and shiny objects. Now think about where this pattern is causing friction inside your organization:

- Are you moving too slowly because everyone is spread too thin, juggling too many projects?
- Are decisions being made—and then un-made, because people don't have the capacity to follow through on commitments?
- Is burnout rampant?
- Are you tolerating the pet projects of senior leaders even though they can be strategically distracting?

Keep asking questions like this until you've identified the most prominent examples of culture friction. That will be your guide for determining what needs to change to improve your culture.

Get Unstuck

Chapter 6 provides the full playbook model for culture change, but above you can see that Matchbox ran their own plays to overcome Heavy Agility:

- Creating a fluid strategic framework rather than a static strategic plan [process]
- Using data analysis as part of rewriting job descriptions [talent/HR]
- Bringing customers more actively into product design [process]

And that's just the beginning. Here are some plays other organizations have used to address the Heavy Agility pattern.

- **After action reviews.** Post-project debriefs with everyone involved to identify areas for improvement. [process]
- **Project Sunsetting Process.** Develop an explicit process for reviewing existing projects and identifying which ones need to be discontinued and by when. [process]
- **Meeting protocols.** Develop protocols for more effective meetings, enabling faster and more transparency decisions. [process]

Can you think of other culture plays that would work for you? Go to culturechangemadeeasybook.com where you'll find a place to browse more plays and submit your own ideas and experiments.

CHAPTER 5

Incomplete Innovation

BOTTOM LINE

Organizations that suffer from Incomplete Innovation value the concepts of innovation more than they value practices of innovation.

- We excel at creating cultures that encourage creativity and a focus on the future. We are not stuck in the past or doing things the way we've always done them. We want to create new value.
- We struggle, however, with the practices of innovation, like running experiments, taking risks, or testing new ideas. We fear making mistakes and we won't risk looking incompetent in front of our peers.
- The competing commitment behind this pattern is a commitment to creating new value, neutralized by a commitment to being right and appearing competent all the time. These organizations genuinely want innovation, but they are afraid to do what it takes, and as a result, they fail to capture new value and lose ground on their competition.

The problem with this Culture Pattern is that it creates value-creation gaps that result in slow growth.

- Employees fall back on what they know and don't explore new ground, so improvement is incremental at best.
- In today's fast-paced environment, slow growth can be deadly.

The solution to this problem is to improve change management, develop psychological safety, and design your workplace to support exploration and connection.

- Organizations that overcome this pattern not only do the basics of change management well, but they are also careful to build a culture that supports agency among employees and de-emphasizes control.
- They invest in creating an environment of psychological safety, where people speak up, take risks, and confront difficult conversations.
- They also intentionally design their workplace (both in-person and virtual) to encourage exploration and connection with people outside their immediate areas.

How you can solve it:

- See your pattern: identify the specific areas where culture friction is messing with success, like slow growth because people wait for things to be perfect, or missed opportunities because people won't try new things.
- Get unstuck: run culture plays like implementing innovation days, providing a budget for taking risks, and recognizing risk takers.

We Won World War Two with Science

According to author Safi Bahcall, "Had there been prediction markets in 1939, the odds would have favored Nazi Germany." And that wasn't based on the number of aircraft, ships, or troops either side had. It was because the Allies were losing what Churchill called a "secret war," which was the race for better technology.[1]

In some instances, technology proved to be a savior for the Allies early on. Having secured air supremacy in Europe fairly quickly, Germany set its sights on Britain, expecting an air assault to pave the way for a planned ground invasion. But Britain was ahead of the game with their advanced research on radar. They were able to spot the enemy squadrons while they were still far away, allowing them to concentrate their attacks. On one day during that campaign, 144 German planes were shot down, compared to only 13 for Britain.[2]

But that radar was not helping them at sea, where Germany's U-boats were wreaking havoc. In addition to sinking warships, the submarines were also taking out tankers and supply ships making their way across the Atlantic to Britain, and that was creating a serious problem. By early 1943, Britain was rationing basic goods at home and was desperately close to running out of oil.

But a team of U.S. scientists helped to turn things around. They developed equipment that allowed bombers to use microwave radar to spot submarine periscopes, even through darkness and clouds, and navigate electronically, rather than by the stars, so they could get where they needed to be without alerting enemy ships. This changed the game. In the month of May of 1943, Allied planes and ships used this new technology to sink 41 submarines—more than in the previous three years combined. Later that year, the German U-boat commander, having withdrawn his fleet, admitted the allies had won "not through superior tactics or strategy, but through

---

1   Safi Bahcall, *Loonshots: Nurture the Crazy Ideas that Win Wars, Cure Diseases, and Transform Industries* (New York: St. Martin's Griffin, 2019), p. 17.

2   ibid., p 27.

his superiority in the field of science."[3]

Bahcall's book, *Loonshots*, chronicles the efforts of those scientists, led by former MIT professor, Vannevar Bush, as well as scientists in the corporate world (specifically, AT&T's Bell Labs), who achieved amazing breakthroughs in relatively short amounts of time, all while experiencing significant resistance from the very organizations that employed them.

That last part is critical. The "powers that be" in the scenarios Bahcall explores all thought these scientists were crazy, promising things that they could never deliver. One of the ways these groups achieved their incredible innovations was by creating an organizational structure that kept the innovators and the "franchise" part of the organization both separate and connected. Bush's Office of Scientific Research and Development (OSRD), which required the approval of the President to be created, was derided by the military as an "end run." That didn't bother Bush, because he knew he couldn't go through the regular channels—he needed the separation. The separation meant the franchise couldn't kill the innovators' projects before they had a chance to get off the ground. But they didn't want to be totally separate either. They intentionally maintained connections to ensure that the innovations could actually be built and used properly in the field. Without balancing the connection and separation, the innovations were at risk.

The lesson here is that innovation must be protected. The heart of innovation is about unlocking new value—obtaining value or achieving benefits that you could never achieve by doing what you already know how to do. It is about discovery. Organizations, however, are very much in love with what they already know how to do. That's the number one focus of the "franchise" part of the organization, and it pays the bills, so it is highly valued. This, in fact, is the genesis of the competing commitment in the Incomplete Innovation pattern. **We are committed to creating new value, but we have a competing commitment to already knowing** the right answer and appearing competent. That leads us to be franchise-heavy, and we fail to provide innovation with the protection it needs.

The Problem: Incomplete Innovation

We are fairly good at talking the talk of innovation, but we are less effective at walking the walk. **We don't create cultures where the practices of innovation are protected, and people end up hesitant to take risks or run real experiments where failure is expected as part of the process.** Some innovation happens along the way, but it's often inefficient, and employee engagement and market share decline as a result. Here is how this Culture Pattern shows up:

- Innovation efforts operate in silos, so they miss key connection points, thus your results are slower and have less impact.
- Market share erodes as innovations delivered by your competitors outpace your continued delivery of what you already know how to do.
- You lose top talent because they eventually become weary of being unable to try new things and discover new value.
- Employees are afraid of getting in trouble if they fail, so they play it safe, and growth is slow.

This is what Incomplete Innovation looks like in the real world. We do believe that innovation is conceptually very important, and that gives us the illusion that we are committed to innovation, but we are not meeting our obligation to protect the work of innovation, and results suffer.

What is Incomplete Innovation?

Organizations with the Incomplete Innovation Culture Pattern value the concepts of innovation more than they value the practices of innovation.

In other words, they ask their people to be creative and future-focused, even to "hack" existing processes, but they fall behind when it comes to taking real risks, running experiments, or beta testing products or services.

The pattern is driven by a competing commitment, where organizations have a strong commitment to creating new value for their customers and stakeholders, but that is neutralized by the commitment they have to *being right and appearing competent*. That means they shy away from risks or trying things they don't already know how to do. As a result, the value they unlock through their innovation efforts is underwhelming, and opportunities to make competition irrelevant are missed.

The aggregate data from our culture assessment reveals the pattern clearly. Employees report consistently that they are able to exercise creativity in their jobs, which is obviously critical for innovation. They are also focused on the future and are wary not to fall into the "we have always done it that way" trap. But the questions focused on the practices of innovation (risk-taking, experimentation, and testing new ideas) scored noticeably more traditional, meaning they are not as present in the culture.

How Incomplete Innovation Shows Up: Value Creation Gaps

The business press has many stories of companies that completely missed the ball on innovation and suffered disastrous results. Kodak, Blockbuster, Blackberry, and Nokia are some of the big ones. Kodak literally invented the digital camera in the 1970s, but declared bankruptcy a few decades later having failed to adapt to the digital age. Blockbuster lost out to Netflix and streaming, and Blackberry and Nokia were industry leaders that failed to ride the smartphone wave.

These companies tend to be written off as ones that simply couldn't see the future, but it is not that simple. Remember, it's easy to see the storyline looking backward, but there were plenty of moments in the past when the future trajectory of these companies and their competitors was not crystal clear. It was in those moments that these companies failed to seize the opportunities for new value creation that were presented to them.

Blockbuster saw the streaming opportunity, for example, but they chose to fall back on what they already knew, and as a result, they failed to capture the value that was in front of them. That's a value creation gap, and in Blockbuster's case, it eventually led to bankruptcy.

Fortunately, most value creation gaps are not that catastrophic. Let's take a look at your marketing department, for example. One of the tools marketing has been using for a long time is A/B testing. Take two small segments of your list, send one message to the A segment, and a different message to the B segment, and then measure the response rates. Whichever did better will be the message you send to the rest of your list. It's not a huge innovation, but it is a good example of the practice of testing new ideas.

Yet some marketing departments are hesitant to do this. As they discuss the A/B testing option, some will express concern that people won't like the B version as much, and it could alienate part of their market. The safer option, they argue, is to just go with the A messaging because it's more familiar.

That's a micro version of the decision Blockbuster made. The marketing department chose not to explore new opportunities, so they missed their chance to unlock some new value (increased engagement from their email list, and perhaps some new sales). This doesn't kill your company instantly, but it offers a great opportunity for your competitors to sneak ahead of you.

Value creation gaps can even show up inside of some relatively successful innovation efforts. We know an organization that was making progress on their innovation efforts, but were still unsatisfied with their results. As they dug deeper, they realized that employees were still being influenced by that competing commitment to appearing competent and having the right answers, so while every department was working on innovation, they did it without making their work visible to the other departments. In the end, they had multiple teams that were creating some new value, but in a completely disconnected way. If they had shared their innovation efforts with each other earlier on, they would have found opportunities to combine efforts and generate a much bigger impact.

It's not just missed opportunities, either. Consistent value creation gaps will make retaining your top talent more difficult. No one likes working for an organization consistently leaving money on the table. The top talent notices when you continuously fall back on the way you've always done things, and they don't like it. They notice that growth is either incremental or nonexistent, and even if they end up staying with you, they'll likely start phoning it in and giving you closer to the bare minimum. Engagement always drops in organizations where success is inhibited, and Incomplete Innovation can definitely drive that.

Avoiding these negative outcomes will require you to establish the right level of protection of your innovation efforts, and that means you'll need to understand the detailed dynamics of how the Incomplete Innovation Culture Pattern works.

Breaking the Pattern Down: Innovation Concepts v. Innovation Practices

Like all Culture Patterns, organizations excel at one part and struggle with another. **For innovation, we excel at the concepts of innovation, but we struggle with the practices.**

Where we Excel: Innovation Concepts

In the early stages of traditional management, even the concepts of innovation were generally not on a leader's radar—it was relegated to the R&D people, or ignored altogether. Early on, in fact, the term *invention* was used rather than innovation—it was about those R&D people literally coming up with new inventions that could be sold or deployed for the public good (such as microwave radar over the Atlantic). For decades, large organizations pursued innovation under the term "diversification." It was about launching new ventures that they hoped would become profitable.

Academia started weighing in on business-related innovation in the late 1970s. Business school professor Rita Mcgrath points to a 1979 Harvard Business Review article as the first to provide academic research on what makes new ventures successful.[4] At that point, the focus was still on large organizations and launching new business ventures. As the 20th century came to a close, however, technology became a bigger part of invention, and the focus shifted from new ventures to product innovation. Then with the advent of the internet, innovation became a household word.

Today, nearly every organization will claim that they do at least some innovation. Tech companies might declare that innovation is part of their DNA, but small businesses, nonprofits, government agencies, service organizations—they all benefit from unlocking new value, so they want innovation to happen. That is why in our culture assessment the three building blocks that are about the concepts of innovation score higher (averaging 3.88, which is 4th among the 16 Culture Pattern components):

- Future focus
- Inspiration
- Creativity

You can't achieve innovation without embracing its underlying concepts. Since we're talking about being able to do things that you currently don't know how to do, then those concepts include focusing on the future (rather than holding onto the past), doing work and achieving results that are inspirational, and anchoring your work in creativity, rather than following recipes and repeatable processes.

If you do the concepts of innovation well in your culture, **you will have created an environment where forward motion is valued. People will continuously have their eyes on how much the organization is resting on its laurels and how much it is trying to move to the future.** Even if a product is selling well and growing, there will still be a team trying to spot market trends that could open up opportunities for a new product, or at least a new take on the existing one. These cultures don't spend too much time perfecting "best practices," and would rather identify new and improved

---

4 https://hbr.org/2012/10/a-brief-history-of-inventing-innovation Accessed October 2023.

solutions that will bring them to the future.

Striving for the future also implies a certain amount of inspiration, and cultures that do the concepts of innovation well understand this. It is not about being "rah rah" and telling inspirational stories that bring tears to your employees' eyes. It is about understanding that the act of reaching value that was previously unreachable is truly important work. These cultures systematically share success stories, reminding everyone of why they do the work. They believe that impact and growth are important, not just for the bottom line, but because of the difference the organization makes both inside and outside its walls.

Innovation also requires that you do more than give lip service to the concept of creativity. Organizations that truly embrace creativity are serious about it. It goes beyond random brainstorming sessions or having toys spread out on the tables of your staff retreat to spur creative thinking (though there is nothing wrong with any of that). These organizations create time and space for creative activities, and they are careful not to micromanage. There is no point in coming up with creative solutions if the boss is just going to make you do it their way in the end.

Concepts alone, however, are necessary but not sufficient. You must also build capacity for the practices of innovation, and that is where most cultures fall short.

Where We Struggle: Innovation Practices

Just as there is a short list of classic innovation failures, there is a lot of attention in the business literature to companies known for excelling at the practice of innovation: Apple, Google, Amazon, Netflix, Tesla, etc. We are not going to write much about these companies in this book, however, because 99% of our readers will respond with, "Yeah, but we're not _____ [fill in the blank from the previous list] and we don't have a zillion dollar innovation budget." We get it. We actually agree that you shouldn't try to duplicate the cultures that you read about in the business press. Instead, try to pull out the principles that drive successful innovation at those companies.

One of those principles is driving out fear. Again, we talked about fear a decade ago in *Humanize*:

> We have been decrying fear in organizations for a long time.
> Peter Drucker and W. Edwards Deming both wrote about
> driving fear out of organizations to improve performance.
> More recently, Jeffrey Pfeffer and Robert Sutton, authors
> of *The Knowing-Doing Gap...*, documented fear's nega-
> tive impact on performance in organizations, arguing that
> it prevents people from taking action that they know they
> should take.[5]

Fear, unfortunately, was a cornerstone of traditional management,
and we are struggling to abandon it inside workplace cultures, even in the digital age. We convince ourselves that fear is a good motivator, and we are blind
to the negative effects that fear has on innovation.

Nowhere is this more evident than in the data from our culture assessment. The three Building Blocks that make up the innovation practices side
of this pattern are all highly impacted by fear:

- Experimentation
- Risk taking
- Testing new ideas

These three Blocks combined averaged only 3.46, 12th among the 16 pattern components. Testing new ideas was particularly traditional, individually
ranking 56th out of 64. **All three of these Blocks are about actually doing
innovation, as opposed to just thinking about it, and while most cultures
do these things to some extent, they don't do them enough.** Why? Because
we're afraid.

Experimentation is about trying things where you intentionally don't know
what the outcome will be. You are testing a hypothesis, and the purpose
of the experiment is to learn from the results, and that includes experiments
that fail. If you're running experiments, and they all succeed, then you're doing

---

5   Notter and Grant, *Humanize* (2012), p. 220.

them wrong—you're only doing things you already know how to do. Proper experiments bring an expectation of some instances of failure because that's where you learn what is wrong with your hypothesis. In the end, however, most of us are afraid to fail. We don't want to try a different way of implementing that project and have it work out badly. **The competing commitment to appearing competent is too strong, so experiments are rare in many workplace cultures.**

Risk-taking triggers the same fear, thus it is similarly rare. **By definition, risk-taking requires that we make ourselves vulnerable, but in most cultures vulnerability is not rewarded.** It may not be stated explicitly, but making yourself vulnerable is viewed as a mistake. Intentionally stepping into an area where you may not have the right answer is considered almost irresponsible. Rather than being enthusiastic about the potential rewards that come from taking risks, our cultures over-emphasize the negative possibilities. It's no wonder that risk-taking scores 48th out of the 64 Blocks.

Testing new ideas is about running beta tests or developing prototypes of possible products and solutions that we share with key stakeholders ahead of time in order to get feedback. The idea of sharing something that is unfinished—by definition, imperfect—with the people who matter is anathema to us. All we can imagine are the negative reactions from stakeholders, and them viewing us as incompetent. As with risk-taking, our cultures emphasize the negative possibilities rather than focusing on the valuable learning that comes with testing new ideas. Again, testing new ideas scores 56th out of the 64 Blocks.

How to Fix Incomplete Innovation

The good news is, fixing this pattern won't require us to learn many new things. Everyone knows how to take risks, run experiments, and test new ideas. It is not a lack of knowledge that is inhibiting innovation. Nor is it about a lack of commitment to innovation from leadership. We see plenty of leaders imploring their employees to run more experiments and devote more effort to innovation, but it's not happening, because **we're not creating the right cultural container for innovation. We're not providing the right soil in which innovation can grow.** We're not providing the right raw materials to build our innovation house. Or pick your own metaphor: the point is, it's the environment that is stifling innovation, so that's what we need to fix.

Unfortunately, that leads too many people to think they need to be like Google if they want to innovate, and that's not true. Google obviously created a cultural container that supported innovation, but they are not the only model. We'll bet that you didn't know that AARP, one of the largest nonprofits in the world with more than 5,000 employees, is a leader in innovation.

AARP is a nonprofit organization that "empowers people to choose how they live as they age," focusing on people 50 years old and up. Headquartered in Washington, DC, they offer a wide range of programming, including advocacy, publications, and research—programs you would expect to see in most membership organizations.

What is very much unlike most membership organizations, however, is AARP's more disciplined approach to innovation. For example, they run a program called "Innovation Labs," where they partner with tech startups to help them develop successful technologies related to health care that are of critical importance to the fifty-plus crowd.[6] They worked with VRHealth, for example, which uses virtual reality to allow patients who have had strokes or other disabling events to do physical therapy at home, and Rendever, which entertains and engages residents of long-term care facilities with virtual reality experiences.

When the pandemic hit, reliance on technology spiked for everyone, including senior citizens. So AARP jumped on the issue and created the "AgeTech Collaborative" in November of 2021, a platform that connects thinkers, entrepreneurs, investors, and other collaborators focused

---

6 https://www.aarp.org/about-aarp/innovation/aarp-innovation-labs.html Accessed October 2023.

on technology products related to aging.[7]

That doesn't sound like your traditional nonprofit membership organization, does it? AARP knows that technology plays a vital role in being able to choose how we live as we age, but they're not merely advocating for investment in technology, they're helping to make it happen. By directly supporting the innovation in the technology space, they are helping to unlock the value that their members will access.

AARP proves that you don't have to be a tech company to master innovation, and when you look at some of their practices (along with several other organizations that we will use as examples in this chapter), you will see that there are three key elements inside your culture that must be addressed if you want to ensure that the practices of innovation are valued as much as the concepts:

- Change readiness,
- Psychological safety, and
- Workplace design.

Change Readiness

We were a bit hesitant to include a reference to change readiness in this chapter because it felt almost too obvious. By definition, innovation involves change; therefore, it seems redundant to say we need to get ourselves ready for change in order to do innovation. **But we are not talking about the tactics of change management here. We're talking about the container you are creating that will support innovation.** Change management tactics include areas like leadership alignment, stakeholder engagement, celebrating success, etc. and yes, you should master those.

You must understand, however, that change management tactics do not create an environment. Change readiness is about that environment,

7   https://www.aarp.org/home-family/personal-technology/info-2021/age-tech-
    collaborative.html Accessed October 2023.

and it refers to specific elements in your culture that should be in place if you want to be good at change (and innovation).

There are two areas your culture must develop to be ready for change: supporting agency, and de-emphasizing control.

Agency refers to how your culture supports individuals at all levels in taking action and making decisions. Cultures with high levels of agency will see people moving forward, asking for forgiveness rather than permission, and backing up other people who want to take action.

Control is essentially the inverse of agency. It refers to the level of control that the leaders in an organization exercise as they manage the organization's affairs, and for change management to be most effective, you want to skew towards lighter levels of control. Cultures that de-emphasize control don't let everyone do anything they want, but they do have leaders who give employees space and decision-making leeway, who make it easy to get resources, and who know when to get out of the way.

Agency and control can be measured. We did not design our culture assessment with change readiness in mind, but we started to see the potential for using it that way when we were working together with an IT consulting firm on a big digital transformation project. The project was planned to run for over a year, but in the first few months it was already running off the rails.

The senior leaders were part of the kickoff meeting where key decisions were made and roles and responsibilities were clarified, but once the change started happening, it ruffled some feathers among staff who were annoyed at how the technology change was causing some friction for them. Some of those employees shared their negative feedback with the senior leaders, and as a result, the leaders began to insert themselves into the process more and more, even reversing some of the decisions they had made previously and taking authority away from the levels below them. In other words, they emphasized control and they were not supporting agency.

Based on this and other, similar experiences the IT consulting firm had been through, we worked with them to identify the specific Building Blocks in our assessment that best measured a culture's capacity for de-emphasizing control and supporting agency. We identified 36 Building Blocks in total, 19 for control and 17 for agency, and they are spread evenly across all of our eight Culture Markers.

For example, the Culture Marker of Agility is focused on change in general, but the two Building Blocks that are specifically focused on de-emphasizing control are *assignment of responsibility* and *leadership facilitation.* Leadership facilitation is about how much leaders get out of the way so more can get done. In the failed digital transformation project that was the heart of the problem. In our aggregate data, that block scores 3.47 (49 out of 64).

The two Building Blocks within agility that are specifically about agency are *decision-making and problem-solving,* and *distribution of power.* Decision-making and problem-solving is about whether or not people can make decisions, even if they are not in charge. Similarly, distribution of power is about relying on expertise more than title or tenure, meaning people with expertise will speak up, and they will be listened to, even if their title isn't as impressive. These were also issues in the failed digital transformation project, and the two blocks do fall well below the median in our aggregate data as well.

Change (and innovation) happens more easily in cultures with high agency and light control. Even if you're doing the basics of change management right (aligning leadership, engaging stakeholders, etc.), a lack of agency means that when the rubber meets the road and action needs to happen—it doesn't. People wait for permission, or they hold back because people more senior to them are in the room, and opportunities to implement the change either don't happen or they happen too slowly. Too much control ends up creating bottlenecks, eroding trust, and reducing staff's capacity to make effective decisions.

When agency and control are done right, however, people take action and the change gets implemented. AARP provides an example of this. In 2017, they created a community called Girlfriend, which produces content for Gen X women. Over the period of a few years, they grew that community to over 1 million participating women.

To build on that success, Shelley Emling, AARP's executive editor of specialized content, had the idea of creating a new Book Club program for the community, and once she had the idea, she didn't hesitate to get started (i.e., she had the agency), and her manager did not insist on too much control. "I was able to go to my boss and say, 'We need to launch a Girlfriend book club because I think there's a lot of readers out there, and this could be a service to people," Emling explained. "She said, 'Go for it.' And now we have 55,000 members."[8] Employees taking action and managers getting out of the way to let it happen—that is critical to implementing the changes that go along with innovation. It also reflects on the second area you will need to develop: psychological safety.

Psychological Safety

A critical component of a container that will support innovation practices is the ability to share concerns or mistakes openly. **There is no innovation without failure, but if people are afraid to talk about failure, then innovation will never happen.** Sharing concerns and mistakes is at the heart of how Harvard Business School Professor Amy Edmondson defines psychological safety:

> When people have psychological safety at work, they feel comfortable sharing concerns and mistakes without fear of embarrassment or retribution. They are confident that they can speak up and won't be humiliated, ignored, or blamed."[9]

It is very unlikely that Emling, in the AARP example above, would have gone to her boss with a risky and unproven idea without an environment of psychological safety in the AARP workplace.

8 https://www.washingtonpost.com/creativegroup/aarp/a-workplace-that-merges-innovation-and-purpose-how-aarp-does-it/ Accessed October 2023.
9 Amy C. Edmondson, *The Fearless Organization: Creating Psychological Safety in the Workplace for Learning, Innovation, and Growth* (Hoboken, NJ: John Wiley and Sons, 2019), p. xvi.

As a researcher on this topic, Edmondson came into the field almost by accident. She was researching team performance in hospitals and had collected an extensive data set related to errors made in the hospitals and the strength of individual teams. Her hypothesis, as you might expect, was that the stronger teams would make fewer errors than the weaker teams, but the data showed the exact opposite. It was the stronger teams that made more mistakes.

So she dug a little deeper and discovered that the stronger teams were not necessarily making more mistakes—they were simply talking about and reporting them more often.[10] In other words, the stronger teams were consistently creating an environment of psychological safety, where everyone on the team could point out mistakes (or possible mistakes) without worrying about getting in trouble or experiencing negative repercussions.

In those teams, mistakes represented opportunities for learning rather than being a cause for punishment or reprimand. In teams that lack psychological safety, employees generally will not speak up about mistakes because they know there will be negative consequences. In those environments, it is much harder to maintain quality and performance.

Google completed an extensive internal study of team performance (code-named Project Aristotle) in 2016. Through detailed data analysis, they identified five factors that explain team performance: clear goals, dependable colleagues, personally meaningful work, a belief that the work has impact, and psychological safety. However, according to the leader of the project, psychological safety was the most important. It was the "underpinning" of the other four.[11]

The negative impact of the lack of psychological safety has also been extensively researched. Perhaps the most disastrous example was how the culture at NASA contributed to the two Space Shuttle disasters—Challenger in 1986 and Columbia in 2003. In the case of Columbia, engineers had grave concerns that the "foam strike" that happened upon take-off could pose a major threat upon reentry (as it eventually did), but those concerns were

---

10 *ibid.*, p.10.
11 *ibid.*, p. 41.

never shared with senior management because the culture did not allow for dissent, particularly with people higher up in the hierarchy. As one Shuttle astronaut described the culture, "At senior levels, during the 1990s, dissent was not tolerated, and therefore people learned if you wanted to survive in the organization, you had to keep your mouth shut."[12]

Psychological safety is particularly important for innovation to be successful. Several studies of research and development teams have shown that teams with greater psychological safety performed better than those without it. The researchers emphasized the importance of psychological safety for teams in R&D "because they necessarily have to take risks and confront failure before they achieve success."[13]

Remember that in our data, the lower-scoring Building Blocks in Innovation were around risk-taking, experimentation, and testing new ideas. These practices are all nearly impossible in the absence of psychological safety. A big piece of creating that safety is making it okay for people to fail.

The startup world has known about this concept for many years. In the 2000s, a group in Silicon Valley started "FailCon," a conference for entrepreneurs and startups that was dedicated to preparing that community for failure. At the time, most conferences were celebrating the successes of the startup community, and the organizers were trying to promote the idea that failure is an opportunity for learning and growth even though failure was still a "taboo topic all over the world."[14]

But you don't have to be a startup to embrace and even celebrate failure internally. Writing in *Inc.*, Annabel Acton extolled the virtues of holding "Idea funerals" as a way to make failure more acceptable.[15] Not all ideas work,

12 Michael Roberto, *Why Great Leaders Don't Take Yes for an Answer: Managing for Conflict and Consensus,* 2nd Edition (Upper Saddle River, NJ: Pearson Education, 2013) p. 83.

13 Edmonson (2019), p. 40.

14 https://thefailcon.com/about.html Accessed October 2023.

15 https://www.inc.com/annabel-acton/stop-talking-about-celebrating-failure-and-start-doing-it-with-these-4-ideas.html Accessed October 2023.

and when you finally pull the plug on that idea that's not working, there is a natural tendency to want to look the other way, redirecting attention away from the failure and towards the things that are working. But taking the time, even in a light-hearted way, to hold a wake for that idea that didn't pan out sends a strong message to people that failure is a part of the job, and it gives the team the opportunity to learn from the failure and maybe even pull out some pieces of the original idea that may still have promise.

FailCons and idea funerals are both situations where people can have a conversation that ultimately makes them a little uncomfortable, which is another key component of a psychologically safe environment: the ability to manage conflict and have difficult conversations.

In theory, conflict is a good thing, particularly for change and innovation. It is resolving the conflict between the status quo and where we want to go that enables change to happen. Unfortunately, in most organizations we avoid conflict like the plague.

Many people avoid conflict because they dislike it. It has produced negative outcomes for them in the past, or they associate it with anger, yelling, or even violence. Others don't mind conflict or even like it and get energized by it, but this group tends to want the conflict to be over quickly. The result is we either avoid the conflict altogether (which inevitably makes it worse), or we only resolve it halfway to finish it quickly (and that allows it to become worse as well). And once the conflict worsens, we all tend to avoid it, and the cycle continues.

To break that cycle, your people need to be good at having conflict conversations. One of the secrets to good conflict conversations is to have them early on. When you get that email from a colleague that rubs you the wrong way, message them and set up a time to talk about it, either in person or by video call. (Note, do NOT have the conflict conversation by email. EVER.) If you wait, you give time for the conflict to grow and become more complex, and you miss the opportunity to resolve it when it is easy.

You also need to be able to get under the surface during conflict conversations. In negotiation, this is called getting at the interests below the positions. Let's say two people share an office, and one wants the window open, but the other wants it closed. Their positions are incompatible, and there really isn't a compromise, as the window is either open or closed—there's nothing in between. In a good conflict conversation, you would spend time talking about why the parties hold those positions. It turns out one wants fresh air (window open), but the other just wants to avoid the draft (window closed). Once you understand the interests—the reasons why—you can find a new solution that meets both parties' interests, like opening a window in a nearby office, so fresh air is circulating without a direct draft.

In more complex conflict conversations, teams could benefit from using the "ladder of inference" that we mentioned in Chapter 2, part of the "accessible mindset" that AAE built into their approach to hierarchy. It is a framework for slowing a conversation down (which is key to having a tough conflict conversation) and looking at the assumptions, meaning, and data that underlie people's conclusions. None of us has a complete picture of the world, and by sharing some of our internal processes about how we make sense of things, we often reveal the key elements that will lead to a resolution of the conflict.

Creating an environment of psychological safety takes time and effort, and you may get some resistance. People don't want to take the time out of their busy work day to talk about failures or participate in conflict resolution training. But investing in psychological safety is critical if you want to reap the rewards of successful innovation.

Workplace Design

Change readiness and psychological safety are relatively widely known to support innovation, but the third area that supports the practices of innovation is perhaps a little more surprising: workplace design. As you think about it, however, what could have more of an impact on the container within which innovation operates than the literal physical container in which your employees work?

The first time we saw this in practice was at the American Society for Surgery of the Hand (ASSH), one of our case studies in *When Millennials*

Take Over. When they bought a building and had the opportunity to redesign everything from scratch, they specifically had innovation in mind. An entire room in their office was named the "innovation ranch," with bright colors, comfortable seating, and a number of non-obvious design features (including a bunk bed). It was designed to spur creativity and help employees see and think about things differently. The rest of the office was designed to give employees lots of choices about where they work, including tread desks for exercising, a small café-like set up for small conversations, quiet concentration in the yoga room, and WIFI on the roof so they could work outside.

Interestingly, AARP seems to have done something similar with part of their office space. Their Innovation Lab is housed in a 10,000-square-foot space they call the "Hatchery," referring, we assume, to hatching new ideas and innovations. The design appears to be nothing like a traditional office, and it also includes bright colors and a variety of space options for doing work.[16]

Some of you, however, may be rolling your eyes right now, because the image of cool spaces with couches and shared work tables sounds like the "open office" idea, which has many proponents, but an equal (or perhaps greater) number of very vocal opponents.

While the concept of an open office has been around since the 1960s, it experienced a resurgence after 2005, when Google redesigned its offices, embracing the open plan concept. Facebook made a similar move a few years later, and since the cool kids were doing it, a lot of other organizations followed suit. The idea was to put everyone in one large space together, which would increase interaction and collaboration. As you take down the walls, there literally could be no silos, people argued.

Not too long after it became popular, however, there was a backlash. Some studies showed that face-to-face communication literally dropped in open office environments, and employees experienced more stress and a literal

---

16 https://www.aarp.org/about-aarp/innovation/aarp-innovation-labs.html Accessed October 2023.

rise in blood pressure.[17] Instead of the collaborative nirvana employees were promised, they ended up frustrated by the constant distractions and lack of privacy.

The debate, quite frankly, frustrated us. It seems to ignore the design maxim of "form follows function." An open design will not work for certain types of work or with certain types of people, but it can be very effective if the context is right. Organizations like ASSH and AARP likely embraced open design specifically in order to promote innovation, and, in fact, there is some research to back them up.

A group called Humanyze (no relation to our first book) conducted research using employee badges that tracked movement and interactions, and they found that open office plans were effective at encouraging interaction specifically within teams that were creating new products or services.[18]

In another study,[19] professor Alex "Sandy" Pentland used similar devices to identify what he called the three elements of successful communication:

- Engagement—interacting with people within your immediate social group
- Exploration—interacting with many people in other social groups
- Energy—increasing your interactions overall.

Different office designs will naturally emphasize these elements of communication differently. Traditional office design (offices and cubes with small group spaces) emphasizes engagement—interacting within your immediate team—and that can be very effective in some cases. A call center, for example, is not going to need open, collaborative space—they rely on cubes, offices, and more privacy—though a large break room where they can interact with

17 https://www.mute.design/2021/12/07/open-office-concept-fixed/ Accessed October 2023.

18 Katherine Schwab, "Everyone Hates Open Offices. Here's Why They Still Exist," *Fast Company*, https://www.fastcompany.com/90285582/everyone-hates-open-plan-offices-heres-why-they-still-exist Accessed October 2023.

19 Ben Waber, Jennifer Magnolfi, and Greg Lindsay, "Workspaces That Move People," Harvard Business Review, https://hbr.org/2014/10/workspaces-that-move-people Accessed October 2023.

their colleagues could help with intra-team information sharing.

But too much emphasis on engagement can be detrimental to innovation, because it gets in the way of the second element, exploration—connecting with others and exploring new ideas. Innovation is ultimately about discovery—finding solutions that are not already within the accepted rules of the game. It's hard to do that without diversity, and exposure to different ways of seeing things. So if an open design can support that kind of exploration, then it makes sense that this design is common among organizations that emphasize innovation.

But there is more to designing a dynamic workspace that supports innovation than getting rid of offices and cubes. Gensler is a leading architecture firm that has been doing research on the impact of office design on individual and organizational performance for many years. In 2016, they zeroed in on innovation.[20] Their annual workplace survey collects data from employees about how their office space is designed and used, but they also collect other data, including the employees' perception of how innovative their company is. Gensler then connected the dots and identified nine specific factors of workplace design that contribute to improved innovation.

The ability to easily meet with others was one of them, and their research confirmed what we cited above—an open office facilitates more of those interactions. But there were other factors as well, including:

- choice
- noise management
- access to outdoor spaces

When we wrote about ASSH in *When Millennials Take Over*, we were highlighting the way they designed their office space around the needs of employees, and that has choice at the very center. Employees do have desks that are their own, but they can choose to work in multiple settings in the office. Gensler found that employees at the most innovative companies were 3 times as likely to have access to a desk that converts from sitting

---

20 Gensler. "U.S. Workplace Survey 2016: Key Findings and Extended Report" (PDF).

to standing (and they also have that at ASSH). Even small adjustments like that can have an impact on innovation. The marketing team ended up doing much of their work in the sitting area by the entrance, for example. This is a critical component of open office design that is often overlooked. It's not just forcing everyone to sit at communal tables. You have to offer multiple spaces where people can go to do their work in ways that meet their needs.

Part of that choice includes being able to work in quiet places. As Gensler asserts, managing noise is important for innovation. ASSH designed their café-like space with the intention that it would be a place for small collaborative conversations, but it ended up being the area where people could do their head-down quiet work. If employees need serious quiet, they can work in the yoga room, or one of their several conference rooms. Menlo Innovations also has an open design, and we saw it in action over two days during our research. There are conversations happening across the room, but the noise level never gets too loud. As the CEO pointed out, the sound of work really isn't that distracting.

Both ASSH and AARP's Innovation Lab embrace the open office concept, but open spaces are simply one option for their employees to get work done. Being able to change your vantage point is integral to thinking differently and coming up with outside-the-box solutions.

One of the more surprising findings from Gensler was the need for fresh air. Gensler found that access to outdoor spaces was also much more common in innovative workplaces. In fact, a study by Roger Ulrich found that people in hospitals recovering surgery with just a view of the outdoors required fewer doses of pain medication and less time in the hospital, so perhaps we shouldn't be so surprised after all.[21]

Of course in the post-pandemic environment, we must also consider the role and impact of the home office. Gensler's study was conducted in 2016, so it didn't address the home office factor, but when you look

21 https://www.wework.com/ideas/research-insights/expert-insights/real-science-be-
    hind-innovative-offices Accessed October 2023.

at the findings of the study (and our research as well), it looks like your home office is a lot closer to ASSH's innovation ranch than your office or cube was. When you work from home you can:
- Change your visual field instantly
- Choose to work in a different location
- Easily access outdoor spaces
- Find a quiet place to work (well, sometimes; this is more true for senior staff than junior staff, generally speaking)

It also allows you easier access to breaktime activities, which some argue is critical to supporting creativity.[22] So the good news is, the move to remote work supports individuals in being more creative and coming up with new ideas.

The bad news is that it does create some hurdles when it comes to the collaborative part of innovation. As mentioned above, the open office design supports people in "exploration" where they are interacting with others outside of their immediate social group, but that assumes people are coming into the office. Working at home does not make that impossible, but it seems clear that it's not coming naturally to us.

In Chapter 2 on collaboration, we shared a model for understanding how to support collaboration that included both task-based and relationship-based collaboration, as well as intentional versus organic. That creates 4 boxes to focus on, and we suggested breaking each box into two: in-person, and remote. The box in that 2x2 diagram that is most relevant to collaborative innovation is the one that is both task-based and organic. This is when we are having valuable work conversations, but they weren't planned. So the question we all must answer is, how do we support these organic connections among employees in the remote environment?

We don't think there is a set answer for that (yet). In fact, at this point, the best way to move forward is to engage in the practice of innovation and start experimenting. Try things like:

---

22 Waber et al., *Harvard Business Review.*

- Create unstructured zoom/teams meetings that are explicitly a group working space; a virtual shared table.
- Schedule quick virtual huddles where people can simply share what they're working on. It's likely that after the huddle, people will connect with others for deeper conversations where it's relevant.
- Use a software tool that pairs employees randomly for virtual coffee chats or short video calls.
- Get serious about your internal online community. Put resources into developing it so people are using it more regularly. This can't be "build it and they will come."

Measure how well those experiments work. If they don't work, then maybe you'll need to rethink your office space even more, because the few days a week people are in the office, you'll want them to do that exploration more, and the space should support that.

How You Can Fix This Culture Pattern

A focus on change readiness, psychological safety, and workplace design can help you overcome the pattern of Incomplete Innovation, but they are not the only ways. Here is how to start seeing your patterns so you can get unstuck.

See Your Pattern

The core of the Incomplete Innovation pattern that we identified in our research is that organizations value the concepts of innovation more than they value the practices of innovation, and that was rooted in a competing commitment: the commitment to creating new value is neutralized by a commitment to being right and always appearing competent. Now think about where this pattern is causing friction inside your organization:

- Is your innovation slow since people are unwilling to share until they feel they have perfected things?

- Is your competition gaining ground on you because you focus too much on what you already know how to do?
- Do you miss opportunities for big gains because no one has time or is unwilling to try new things?
- Is the value you're delivering to customers/stakeholders eroding over time?

Keep asking questions like this until you've identified the most prominent examples of culture friction. That will be your guide for figuring out what needs to change to improve your culture.

Get Unstuck

Chapter 6 provides the playbook model for culture change, and we discussed several plays that can be run in the categories of change readiness, psychological safety, and workplace design:

- Create processes for sharing strategy and strategic goals with everyone to enable change readiness [process]
- Provide conflict resolution training for psychological safety [talent/HR]
- Conduct "idea funerals" to make failure more acceptable [process] Redesign office space to be more collaborative and allow for exploration [structure/design]

But that's just the beginning. Here are some plays other organizations have used to address the Incomplete Innovation pattern.

- **Innovation days.** Setting aside a full day, company-wide (not just R&D) to focus on innovation and prototyping [process]
- **Risk-taking budget.** Set aside a certain amount of money in each department for projects that take risks. [process]
- **New idea metrics.** Develop a system for tracking new ideas and the results they generate over time. [process]
- **Recognize good risk-taking behaviors.** Set up a recognition/reward program to publicly acknowledge people who take risks and learn from them. [process]

Can you think of other culture plays that would work for you? Go to culturechangemadeeasybook.com where you'll find a place to browse more plays and submit your own ideas and experiments.

In our next chapter, we will fully explain our playbook model of culture change, now that we have thoroughly covered the four Culture Patterns of Awkward Collaboration, Lagging Transparency, Heavy Agility, and Incomplete Innovation.

As we mentioned in Chapter 1, however, there are eight patterns that emerged from our research. We refer to the four we covered here as the "big four," because we find them to be more prevalent than the others and are more frequently the focus of the action items that organizations develop when they are changing their culture.

But the other four Culture Patterns—Intangible Growth, Micro Inclusion, Shallow Solutions and Incrementally Digital—are still important. We discuss them briefly in Appendix A and they should be on your radar as you look for culture friction inside your organization.

CHAPTER 6

Getting Unstuck: The Playbook Model for Culture Change

BOTTOM LINE

Getting unstuck requires managing your culture continuously by creating a Culture Playbook of "plays"—i.e., things you do differently inside your organization that generate the behaviors that drive success.

- There are 6 sections to your playbook. Most (if not all) culture plays can be categorized in one of these areas, and this is a simple way to start brainstorming them.

    + Process
    + Structure and Design
    + Technology
    + Talent and Human Resources
    + Rituals and Artifacts
    + Culture Stewardship

- You need to balance the plays that work "in" the culture (changing how you do things) and "on" the culture (communicating and nurturing the culture change itself).
- You also want the right balance of quick wins along with "big ideas" (longer-term infrastructure changes).

Everyone, at every level of the organization, can start changing culture tomorrow.

- Don't get overwhelmed; just pick some plays and run them.

Getting Unstuck

If you jumped to this chapter from the end of Chapter 2, welcome! If you just finished all four chapters on the Culture Patterns of Awkward Collaboration, Lagging Transparency, Heavy Agility, and Incomplete Innovation, nicely done! Either way, you've probably realized that at least some of these Culture Patterns apply to your organization in ways that are messing with your success, so you have arrived at the question that everyone has at this point:

What do we do about all this?

The short answer is:

Write up a culture change playbook, then run some culture plays.

Once you figure out the direction you want to move your culture (e.g., to be better at collaboration or innovation), you brainstorm a number of culture plays that you can run—actions you can take, things you can change—that will move the culture in that direction. Then you implement the culture plays, making adjustments along the way, revising plays or bringing in new ones, until you can measurably see that the culture has ended up in that place you wanted it to be.

Yes, it's as simple as that. That's how playbooks work in sports, too.

No matter what sport you're talking about, it's impossible to win by running a single play. You need to run many, which is why teams devote significant energy to developing a good playbook. Some plays are designed to make smaller, incremental gains, while others are higher-risk, with the potential for higher payoff. And many plays don't work out the way they were designed the first time they are applied in a dynamic game situation. Some plays perform badly, so we bring them back, redesign them, and try them again. It's the combination of the right plays and the right people that produce the win. We know it's an overused sports metaphor, but it really works for culture change.

At the end of each of the previous four chapters, we gave you examples of specific plays that our case study organizations or others have run to address the four primary Culture Patterns, including plays like implementing a comprehensive project management system, building out a robust intranet, sharing extensive KPIs internally, or providing training in conflict resolution.

In this chapter, we'll expand on those, giving you a holistic model for a culture change playbook that you can start working on immediately.

Culture Management Maturity Model

A few years ago, we wrote a white paper that lays out a culture management maturity model (see Appendix D for the full text of the paper, if you are interested). It has three stages, based on your organization's overall approach to culture:

1. Culture as a Concept.
2. Culture as a Practice.
3. Culture as a System.

Each stage has two levels.

At the **Culture as a Concept** stage, culture is either Unintended (level 0) or Idealized (level 1). At the unintended level, you are completely ignoring culture, and it's developing organically, on its own. Startups are typically at this level, as are many departments or teams inside an organization that settle for whatever the default culture is. The moment you get intentional about culture, however, your next step is to define what the ideal culture is. This is the level where a lot of core values posters get created. But again, your efforts to manage or change culture are limited to getting clear about and promoting the concepts. Note that both level 0 and level 1 cultures can be either good or bad, or can start off good and then regress into bad (or vice versa), depending on internal factors like the personalities who work there currently, or external factors like the specific business environment in which they operate.

There is a difference between getting intentional about culture and getting serious about it, and if you're serious, you'll start to work on the two levels within the **Culture as a Practice** stage. Level 2 is Designed, and this is the level where you do things like assess your culture and develop a culture change plan. **This whole book is focused squarely on this level,**

and we assume this is where most of our readers either are or want to be. Moving up to Managed (level 3) requires more work on a culture management infrastructure and a shift in approach, from culture as a single project you're working on, to a function that needs continuous management (like finance or HR, for example). You'll be putting in people processes and support for that work at this level.

The most advanced stage, **Culture as a System**, is going to be aspirational for most organizations. The organizations at this stage aren't really managing culture as much as they are living it fully. At level 4 (Embedded) they establish culture firmly in HR, internal and external communications, and some parts of operations (like office space), and at level 5 (Integrated), culture becomes seamlessly woven into areas like strategy and governance.

The reason so few reach the third stage is because they struggle with culture change, so they can't get past level 2 (designed). We know something needs to change but we're not sure what, when, or how to make it happen, or even who can do it. We'd like to change that, so below we give you a model that you can use, no matter what your role is in the organization, to ensure that culture change happens.

The Playbook Model for Culture Change

In culture change, a culture play is simply an action item designed to move the culture in a direction that will make your organization more successful. It can be introducing something new, changing something that already exists in your organization, or stopping something that you're currently doing.

The easiest example we can think of is putting your staff through a training program. Let's say you're having difficulty with collaboration across silos, and there has been a history of conflict between some departments that is making it worse. A good play to run would be a training in conflict resolution. If people had the skills to have better conflict conversations, it would increase the chances of cross-silo collaboration being successful. Any training program is designed to teach people how to do things better or differently, and that's behavior change. When you are changing behaviors, you are changing the culture.

But training is only one kind of play. In our model, there are six different categories for plays in your culture playbook:

- Process,
- Structure and Design,
- Technology,
- Human Resources and Talent,
- Rituals and Artifacts, and
- Stewardship.

Adding a meeting of middle managers is an example of a process play, implementing a company-wide intranet (or using the existing intranet in a different way) is a technology play, and the conflict resolution training program would fall under HR and talent. Everything you can do to change workplace culture will fall into one of these six buckets, and to be successful in culture change, you will likely need plays in all six.

In the Culture Versus On the Culture

There is an important distinction to be made, however, among the six categories. **The first three—process, structure and design, and technology—represent changes in how people get their work done inside the organization. The second three are more related to how the organization sustains and manages the culture itself over time.** It's similar to a distinction that most leaders understand: working "in" the business, versus working "on" the business.

As organizations grow, leaders often find themselves drawn into working "in" the business—focusing on specific products or services, managing the sales process, or handling administrative details. If they focus too deeply on these issues, they don't have time to work "on" the business, which includes setting strategy, building out bigger systems, analyzing broader market trends, or engaging in research and development. If you want to grow or scale your business, then you need to balance your attention in these two areas.

This concept applies to your culture change playbook as well. Working "in" the culture (process, structure/design, technology) is about making changes to the way people do their work. There are an infinite number of changes you can make to the way things are done, but **culture plays are specifically designed to change things in ways that clarify and reinforce what's valued in the culture.** You may constantly be looking for ways to improve how your people use your intranet, but the specific change of creating a space for your marketing and product development groups to collaborate, for example, is a play in your culture change playbook because you're doing it to make clear that collaboration across department lines is important to the success of the organization and therefore a key piece of your culture to be reinforced.

Working "on" the culture (human resources and talent, rituals and artifacts, and stewardship) is about the work we call **culture management.** In addition to changing behaviors among employees, it is important to run culture plays that are designed to manage the growth and development of the culture at a higher level. That includes communicating what your culture is, both internally and externally, managing the implementation of the plays, and measuring the impact. Without this work, the changes you're making "in" the culture can easily lose momentum and focus. You may have a large number of internal training programs, for example, but the conflict resolution training play is designed specifically to build a capacity among employees that would support the shift toward a culture that values collaborative groups.

Making It Real Versus Making It Permanent

In addition to distinguishing between plays that work on the culture versus in the culture, **you must also create a balanced portfolio of culture-change plays with varying degrees of level of effort and impact.**

Some culture change plays are intentionally designed to have a relatively low impact because these plays also typically require a relatively low level of effort. The layman's term for these plays is "low hanging fruit." While relatively easy to implement, these **quick wins play a critical role in culture change, because they make culture change efforts visible to everyone.**

For example, if you were trying to fix the Lagging Transparency Culture Pattern, you could implement a very simple process play: after every senior team meeting, write up the notes and share them with the entire staff (minus anything sensitive or confidential), briefly describing the content of the conversation and documenting any decisions that were made.

This is a very easy play to run. It requires no money, and very little time (since a version of those notes was probably already being prepared for the team itself), and it could be implemented effectively instantly. This play, by itself, will not have a huge impact on your culture. Truth be told, as much as employees often clamor to find out what happens at those mysterious senior management team meetings, they are frequently underwhelmed when they finally see the notes. Those notes will not transform that Lagging Transparency pattern, but they will help at least a little.

The more important value of this kind of low-hanging fruit play is that it serves as a constant reminder that you are working on making the culture more transparent. Each time the senior team meets, the entire staff gets a reminder that this is a priority for the organization and that being more proactive in the sharing of information is a behavior that is valued.

We call this "making it real." If you don't do these visible, low-effort, low-impact plays, then you'll only be left with the longer-term, heavier lifts. Those plays are important too, but you typically don't see the results of those plays until down the road—months, or, in some cases, years later. That means your people will not see the change happening, and they will lose trust. They believed you when you told them that the Culture Pattern of Lagging Transparency was holding everyone back and would be the focus of the culture change. Then a few months later, they seemingly have no evidence of that, so they write it off as another empty promise from management. That is why the "making it real" plays are so important.

That said, if you only focus on the low hanging fruit you will also be in trouble. **You must balance that with the longer-term, heavier impact, "big idea" culture plays that we call "making it permanent." These plays require a significant investment of time, effort, and (frequently) money, but they represent a more significant and lasting change to the culture.**

Without these, if you're only doing quick wins, then employees will likely conclude that you are merely paying lip service to improving your culture, because you're not willing to invest in real change.

For example, in Chapter 2, we talked about AAE's complete overhaul of their project management system, which involved selecting and implementing new enterprise software, designing new project management processes, and getting both training and consulting from an external consulting firm. The whole thing wasn't fully rolled out for almost a year after they committed to the project, but once it was in place, it transformed the way they collaborated across functional areas. That is making it permanent.

So balance is the key, both in terms of in the culture v. on the culture and making it real v. making it permanent.

Now let's take a look inside each of the culture play categories to see what the plays really look like.

Process Plays

When you're changing culture, the process category typically has the most plays in it, because your organization is essentially a big bunch of processes. Processes fall into the following broad categories.

Production and Delivery

These are the processes you use to get the core work of your organization done, so they vary by industry. Manufacturing processes are different from software design processes or event planning processes, but changing these processes can have a big impact on culture, so don't ignore this category. These processes can be related to the creation/design of the products or services, or their delivery/implementation.

For example, both Matchbox Virtual Media (case study in the Heavy Agility chapter) and Menlo Innovations (case study from *When Millennials Take Over*) intentionally designed their core work processes to directly involve customers in an ongoing way, which allowed them to be much more agile.

Sales and Marketing

Any process related to securing revenue falls into this category, including generating leads, closing sales, market research, customer relationship management, branding, advertising, sponsorship, etc.

A simple marketing culture play is to use the way you describe your workplace culture in your marketing campaigns or on your website ("why work with us?") to sell your products and services, NOT just to hire new talent.

Strategy and Metrics

These processes are more related to working "on" the business and include strategic planning, budgeting, research, and anything related to setting metrics to track work and progress, either for the organization as a whole or for specific departments.

In the Lagging Transparency chapter, we talk about how a lack of leading indicator metrics can lead to strategic mistakes, so building more leading indicators into your quarterly planning process is an example of a strategic process change that could help fix that Culture Pattern.

Administration and Support

These are organizational infrastructure processes that support everyone in being able to get their other work done, and these include things like facilities management, bookkeeping and finance, IT, and other operational functions.

Pinion, the case study in the Lagging Transparency chapter, steered away from the tradition of tracking financials by individual offices, for example, in order to promote a culture of "one firm" that enabled people across geographic locations to collaborate more effectively, with less competition. Budgeting is another administrative process that can have a big impact on culture (making that process more transparent can build trust).

Internal Communications

The power of communications is so important it deserves its own section here (if not its own book in the future!). We believe that many (most?) culture problems boil down to bad communication—up and down the hierarchy, horizontally across departments, and between individuals. Often, the low-hanging fruit culture plays you will come up with have to do with communicating better, or defining *how* you communicate better. What's the best way to conduct an all-staff meeting to ensure everyone feels like they are part of the mission of the company? Should this unpopular Friday team meeting really be an email with updates? How could we make it more efficient and get to the meat of what we want to talk about? Could this other email have been a direct Slack message, without the need to cc the world?

Remember, when you are identifying process plays for your culture change playbook, you are not only improving a process, but you are also changing the process in a way that generates the new behaviors that you want to be valued inside your culture. Better communication can be used to improve *all* of the Culture Markers we measure in our data (collaboration, agility, innovation, inclusion, transparency, etc.).

Structure and Design Plays

There are two totally separate aspects of structure and design to consider when coming up with culture change plays: organizational and physical. Organizational structure and design refers to organizational charts, reporting relationships, and hierarchical levels, but you must also consider physical structure and design, meaning how the office or workplace is designed.

Organizational Design

The "reorganization" has long been a tool that management has used to make changes, though employees tend to respond more with sarcasm and frustration than engagement and excitement upon the announcement of a reorg.

One government employee we worked with many years ago joked that their agency's motto should be "Department of [XYZ]: 100 Years of Reorganization." Major reorganizations, however, particularly in large organizations, have typically been less about improving culture and more about internal politics and cost savings. While a full reorganization is an option, we recommend being more subtle and effective with your structure/design plays.

Changing lines on the organizational chart, in fact, is not required. In the Awkward Collaboration chapter, we showed you how AAE improved collaboration by making hierarchy "more accessible." This was about operationalizing a new definition of what the hierarchy lines meant (i.e., they are about decision-making, but not about restricted access) rather than making any changes of who reports to whom. They also championed the use of ad-hoc cross-functional teams that intentionally included people from different levels of the hierarchy, using these teams to implement some of the culture plays that they developed.

Some organizations have chosen to be more radical in reinforcing their culture through organizational structure. W.L. Gore and Associates (the makers of the water-proof Gore-Tex fabric, among other things) got some attention in the management world for its hierarchy with only two titles: leader and associate. What makes it more innovative is they allow the associates to bestow—and take away—their leader's title.

Whether you are traditional or radical, though, it's important to treat your structure plays like experiments. A property management company in Japan was concerned that middle managers were creating a bottleneck in the communication flow, so they instituted some changes that would allow people from different departments to deal with each other more directly rather than through the managers.[1] Their changes worked initially—people were spending less time in meetings and more time getting work done.

A little bit later, however, some quality issues emerged. Communication

---

1   Ethan Bernstein and Ben Waber, "The Truth About Open Offices," *Harvard Business Review*, November-December 2014, https://hbr.org/2019/11/the-truth-about-open-offices Accessed October 2023.

was faster now, but it turns out those middle managers played a critical role in quality control, and the new structure left them out of that process. Remember that structure plays are always a means to an end—there is no one "right" structure. So, as you run these plays, make sure you run them as experiments and are willing to reverse your decision if you find they aren't working the way you planned.

Office Design

We discussed office design extensively in Incomplete Innovation chapter. Organizations both large (AARP) and small (American Society for Surgery of the Hand) have intentionally redesigned all or parts of their office space to promote innovation. We made the case for ignoring the debate about whether offices should be open with shared work tables or traditional with offices and cubes. There is no "right" answer here. Remember, a culture play is something you do to move your culture in one direction or another. Many would blindly claim that open office designs promoted more collaboration, only to find that everyone works side by side with headphones on, not talking to each other. In cases like that, the problem wasn't the design—the problem was misunderstanding how and when people collaborate.

Again, we recommend an experimental approach to your office design plays, in order to make them more effective. Two of the four case studies in our book *When Millennials Take Over* used an open office plan, but two did not (more evidence that there is no right answer). As we mentioned in Chapter 5, ASSH designed their office to give their employees choices in their work environment, including a café-style area with small tables near the kitchen. They thought this space would be used for quick, collaborative meetings with small groups, but, in fact, people ended up using it for their quiet, solo work—and there's nothing wrong with that. All office design plays are experiments, and your goal is to use what you learn from them to make further adjustments, if needed, to ensure the behaviors you wanted more of in your culture are happening.

In the post-pandemic world, the office space conversation has changed once again, now focused on remote work and how much time people should be spending in the office. Some are calling for a complete return to the office, but we don't think we are ever going back to the way it was. Either way, though, we believe you can ignore the high-level debates about this. Instead, stay vigilant with your experiments and focus on the behaviors you want to see in YOUR culture.

AAE (case study in Chapter 2) had moved into a new office in downtown Chicago not long before the pandemic hit. Like everyone else, they figured out how to run a remote office effectively during the lock-down, but when things opened up enough for them to consider returning to the office, they took a simple, experimental approach: they started by all agreeing to come in on Tuesdays. In addition to socializing with each other more, they found that they used their in-person time for meetings. Some meetings work fine on video calls, but some of the larger or more complex conversations are not as effective, so they leveraged their in-person time for the meetings that worked better in person—so much so that they decided to come into the office on Wednesdays as well. Now that they are using those two days for meetings, they are realizing that their office layout (mostly offices and cubes with a couple of conference rooms) is not ideal for how they are using their space now. As a small organization, they are not likely to spend resources on a full redesign, but they are considering new ways of configuring what they have now to support more effective in-person meetings.

Technology Plays

We are in the digital age, so culture change will always have a digital component. Technology culture plays involve deploying new software or making significant changes to the way you use one or more of your current technology solutions, all to generate behaviors that move the culture in the direction of your priorities.

In our 2019 book, *The Non-Obvious Guide To Employee Engagement*, we had a section on how to use technology to improve engagement, and we broke it down into the following categories:

• Intranets and communities

- Collaboration and project management
- Feedback and performance management
- Recognition and rewards
- Innovation

These categories still make some sense, but we've actually pulled back from categorizing, because the landscape is changing too quickly. Many of the tools that we pointed to back in 2019 have pivoted or disappeared. What started as recognition software shifted to employee engagement software and then morphed again to employee experience platforms. And in 2019, we didn't even mention Zoom or Microsoft Teams!

Instead of categories, we'll simply talk about the two areas that are top of mind for most leaders when it comes to technology: collaboration tools and artificial intelligence.

Collaboration Tools

When the 2020 pandemic hit, nearly every organization learned how to run technology plays in the form of video meetings (e.g., Zoom, Teams, Google Meet) and team/chat software (e.g., Teams, Slack). While these tools existed before the pandemic, they have since become the bedrock for communication and collaboration. The move to these technologies was simply a practical necessity at the time, but it had a significant impact on workplace culture. With multiple "channels" of communication visible to everyone in the organization, for example, transparency was impacted.

In some cases, these technologies had a positive impact on inclusion: it is almost impossible to talk over someone on Zoom, and people who had previously been marginalized at in-person meetings could have their voices heard. They also posed some challenges, of course, like maintaining work-life balance in an environment of non-stop zoom meetings, as well as some information overload with so many communication channels available.

Now that these collaboration tools are in place, there are plenty of opportunities to change the way companies use the tools as part of a culture change effort. In Chapter 3, we gave the example of having departments share regular updates on what they are doing, which could enable more effective customer service. We also highlighted the use of a company-wide intranet: Pinion invested heavily in both the technology and devoting staff time to building out the content to make sure employees had a place where they could go to find anything. AAE ran a big technology play by deploying project management software in order to break the Awkward Collaboration pattern. Matchbox used something as simple as Google Docs to help with their internal co-creation. All of this is less about finding a specific type of software than it is about deploying any and all software strategically in service of the culture change.

Generative Artificial Intelligence

As we are writing this book, generative AI is exploding on the scene, and it's causing so much consternation and excitement that we would be remiss not to mention it. Look above at the section on Process Plays, and for every type of play, you can probably come up with a way to inject AI into the process to make it faster or more effective.

The bigger picture impact of AI will be the way it puts power into the hands of every individual employee, and we think that is going to change everyone's culture. AI will do the same thing that computers and the social internet did—give individuals the power to do things only centralized resources could do before—but now with an exponential curve.

Some, of course, do not have such an optimistic view of this AI revolution. There is an emerging question about the value of "human-ness" in the face of AI. As Maddie wrote on our blog,[2]

> The dawn of artificial intelligence (AI) has often been portrayed in stark, dystopian terms: machines overtaking human jobs, algorithms making critical decisions, and a future

---

2 7 Ways the Most Human Workplaces Will Thrive in the Age of AI (propelnow.co)

where human input seems redundant. However, this narrative overlooks the profound beauty and opportunity of being human in this Aquarian age of technological advancement. Far from making us obsolete, I believe AI can serve as a foil, highlighting our uniquely human qualities and amplifying our capabilities, especially in the workplace.

She goes on to identify areas like creativity, collaboration (natch), ethics, meaning and purpose, adaptability, and other human qualities that may rise to the top as our workplaces become more and more AI-enabled. What does this mean for culture? Those human qualities might just end up being some of the culture elements we value the most and need to reinforce per the strategies in this book.

Human Resources and Talent Plays

This category of plays moves us into the plays that work more "on" the culture than "in" it, though this category in particular is a blend of the two. Most of the plays in this category are focused on behaviors. They are designed to ensure that the employees in the organization are displaying the behaviors that the new culture needs to be successful. On the other hand, the plays themselves are not changes to work processes, they are new ways of implementing HR processes, which are more about supporting the organization in getting where it needs to go. There are three main categories of HR and talent plays: talent pipeline, professional development, and compensation and recognition.

Talent Pipeline

When you are changing culture, then you must, almost by definition, make changes to the way you hire and fire employees. The plays in this category are all about culture fit, either when evaluating a potential hire or giving feedback to existing employees. Once you are clear on how you define your culture and how it drives your success, you can modify your talent pipeline processes to keep everyone aligned with your culture. It starts with hiring.

Typical hiring processes are mostly focused on evaluating the skills and knowledge that are required to do the job in question, and culture fit is either ignored, misunderstood as being about "people like us" (we could write a whole other book on the diversity and inclusion issues with this), or given cursory attention. Not so at Menlo Innovations, the software company we've mentioned that uses paired programming (two developers sharing one computer to write code). The Menlo hiring process puts culture first. While they certainly evaluate the technical skills of the candidates, they also believe that it is easier to teach coding skills than it is to teach good collaboration, so that's the focus of the first round of the hiring process. After all, if two people are going to be sharing a mouse, then they'd better be good at collaborating.

The first round in their hiring process starts with a group interview, with as many as thirty people competing for the same position. They put the candidates in pairs and give them a software coding problem to solve—each pair gets one piece of paper and one pencil, forcing them to collaborate. In addition, they are judged not only on the quality of their problem-solving but specifically on how well each candidate helps their partner make it through to the next round. It's quite a tall order to be asked to help a competitor get to the next round when you may end up losing the job to them, but if you are not willing to collaborate that much, then Menlo doesn't want you as an employee.

Performance management is another part of the talent pipeline where you can inject a stronger focus on culture. In our experience, most people hate their system of performance management, which often feels like a gigantic waste of time filling out endless review forms only to have everyone get rated a 4 and given a 2-3% raise at the end of the year. The reasons for that are many, and we're not going to try and solve the bigger performance review problem here, but there is something you can do better when it comes to culture change: focus specifically on behaviors.

An Australian nonprofit identified 12 principles that they felt would improve culture and performance, including things like transparency, relationship building, and decentralization. Then they took each one and wrote up two paragraphs: one describing what it looks like when someone is living that cultural principle well, and another describing what it looks like when they are not. Each paragraph identified specific behaviors to clarify the principle.

They then added a section of their performance review process where everyone was evaluated on all 12 principles, giving red/yellow/green ratings based on both paragraphs for each principle. This wasn't about determining a merit increase—it was about ensuring that more of the behaviors that drove the success of the organization were more present in the culture.

Interestingly, when they rolled out the new system, one of the senior leaders asked to resign. This is something you should be prepared for when you are managing talent with culture fit in mind. A lack of culture fit simply contains an opportunity for that person to find the right fit somewhere else, leaving room for a new person with a more aligned mindset to come into the system. It's also evidence of one of the most important lessons we've learned about culture change over the years: **if you're doing culture change and people aren't leaving, then you're doing it wrong.** It's actually a good thing when cultural clarity pushes people who aren't the right fit to find work elsewhere.

Professional Development

A direct way to promote the behaviors you'd like to see more of in your culture is through training. Previously, we gave the example of training everyone on how to manage conflict and facilitate difficult conversations to help improve cross-functional collaboration. Here are some common categories of training that can be used to support culture change.

Communication and Collaboration, which includes conflict resolution training but could also incorporate improving communication skills more broadly, understanding and applying personality types (e.g., DiSC or Myers-Briggs), or learning the practice of facilitation. Clearer communication is an important and trainable skill, and you could look into a practice launched by the news site Axios called Smart Brevity[3] (your authors' current obsession, which has impacted how we wrote this book[4]), which describes how clear communication that puts the bottom line up front can foster transparency, build trust and lead to more engagement at work.

Diversity, Equity, and Inclusion, which could be any training that helps employees understand and appreciate different perspectives, cultures, and backgrounds. Specific topics include unconscious bias, microaggression, accessibility and disability, and cultural competence.

Leadership Development is a broad training category but could include topics like emotional intelligence, developing a growth mindset, change management, and ethics.

Health and wellness training became popular during the pandemic and includes topics like stress management, building resilience, and burnout prevention for managers.

Technical skills training is often a part of larger culture plays. In Chapter 3, we mention AAE's extensive play around project management, which included rolling out software and a new process for all staff, and a major part of that initiative was training all staff on how to use the software and run the new processes.

We also include coaching and mentoring in the professional development category. The topic areas could be exactly the same as those above, but the delivery mechanism for learning the skills or knowledge is one-on-one conversations either with an outside expert or an internal colleague.

Compensation and Recognition

Culture is fundamentally about what is valued, and where the money goes will usually make that very clear. For example, former Whole Foods CEO John Mackey wanted to create a culture that valued fairness and shared success,

---

3   https://www.axios.com/smart-brevity Accessed October 2023.
4   https://www.axioshq.com/insights/internal-communication-strategies-keeps-teams-better-aligned Accessed October 2023.

so he limited the CEO's salary to no more than 14 times what the low-est-paid employee was paid (if that strikes you as high, the AFL-CIO reports that in 2022 the average ratio among S&P 500 companies was 272 to 1).[5] Forbes was quick to point out that Mackey's stock options are not included in that number, but they did admit that his salary was relatively low and that 93% of the stock options were given to regular employees.[6]

The more common HR culture play related to compensation, however, is about bonuses, specifically when it comes to whether they are based on individual or group performance. In his book *Drive*, author Dan Pink argues that financial incentives naturally create a narrower focus. They work well when the rules of the game are simple, but for complex tasks, the laser focus that bonuses generate results in details get missed, and he argues that performance can actually go down with financial incentives.[7] One study divided employees into two groups, one where bonuses were calculated on individual performance and one where they were based on group perfor-mance, and the people getting individual rewards literally sent fewer emails to their colleagues as they got their work done. So plays related to compen-sation are not just about retaining employees—they can change behaviors related to collaboration and transparency.

In addition to annual bonuses, some organizations implement spot bonuses as a relatively easy culture play, where managers can reward employ-ees for engaging in specific behaviors that are valued by the culture by being able to give a small gift card or other monetary reward on the spot. Other cul-ture plays involve simple ways to recognize and/or reward people who embody the culture well. In fact, the power of recognition for engagement has given rise to companies like Workhuman, a recognition software platform, that are built on the idea that "when people feel seen, they give their all."[8]

5   https://aflcio.org/paywatch/company-pay-ratios Accessed October 2023.
6   https://www.forbes.com/2006/04/20/john-mackey-pay_cx_hc_06ceo_0420wholefoods. html?sh=6e0003857c17 Accessed October 2023.
7   Daniel H. Pink, *Drive: The Surprising Truth About What Motivates Us* (New York: Penguin Group, 2009).
8   https://www.workhuman.com/ Accessed November 2023.

Rituals and Artifacts Plays

This category is about communication—specifically, how you describe what your culture is, both internally and externally. While much of culture is conveyed through everyday conversations among employees, an organization can reinforce cultural messaging by creating artifacts (memorable objects) and rituals (gatherings with symbolic importance) that continuously remind people what the culture is about.

Most artifacts come in the form of documents, slide decks, web pages, or other collateral that communicate the core elements of a culture in a memorable way. **The proverbial core values posters fall into this category, but as we mentioned before, you'd better make sure a one-word core values poster is backed up somewhere with documentation that explains in more detail why that value matters and what it looks like at a behavioral level, in practice.** Adding pages to your externally facing website that describe your culture and what you value are also artifacts.

A more strategic and streamlined approach is to view the collection of these core artifacts as a "culture code." This will allow your internal communications team to develop multiple pieces of collateral that describe the culture in a consistent way and use different types and formats of communication most effectively. In addition to interesting posters to remind people of key concepts, you could have longer documents, like a manifesto, that get into the details. You could have an external webpage that describes your culture to customers, and a more extensive version in your employee handbook that describes it to staff. These artifacts tell a more compelling story about your culture taken together than they do individually—and any inconsistencies will soon be obvious to anyone looking (*cough* Enron[9] *cough*).

Rituals can have some overlap with process and HR/talent plays. For example, the entire onboarding process would fall more under the HR/talent plays, but during that process, there is often some kind of meeting

---

9 https://www.rebelplaybook.com/interviews/values-gone-wrong-enron-corporation Accessed October 2023.

or lunch event to welcome new employees, where elements of the culture are communicated. That's an example of a ritual play.

Similarly, cultural communication is often added to existing meeting processes, like an all-hands meeting or team building activities and retreats. The team building activities have ancillary goals, like building relationships among team members or giving back to the community through volunteering, but they are also intentionally communicating what the culture values to the employees.

Some employee recognition plays would fall into the ritual category as well, like holding ceremonies or events to recognize and celebrate employee achievements. This can include annual award ceremonies, employee of the month programs, etc.

Stewardship Plays

Stewardship plays are squarely about working on the culture, rather than in it. This is the category of plays where you ensure that the culture is continuously and effectively managed over time. Culture, ultimately, needs to be someone's job.

In larger organizations, this can be one or more full-time positions (typically housed within HR). In smaller organizations, the duties might be spread across multiple people in multiple departments, but either way, someone must be responsible for culture design and culture management. There are four broad categories of plays.

Diagnosis

You should always be on the lookout for culture friction—where things aren't going well and you realize that a Culture Pattern or competing commitment is one of the primary causes. There are lots of options for how to do this.

Employee surveys. Running a full culture assessment is perhaps the most obvious choice, as that will clearly identify Culture Patterns and areas of culture friction. But you can also run shorter, pulse surveys with employees or use engagement surveys to focus more on the specific areas where problems occur.

Focus groups and interviews. Qualitative data is just as useful (if not even more so) than quantitative data in identifying areas of culture friction and competing commitments, so you could spend time with your colleagues having open conversations about what the culture is and where it's messing with success.

Review performance data. This is more about identifying the areas of culture friction rather than the underlying cultural issues that cause them, but spend some time analyzing performance metrics, including productivity, employee turnover, and customer satisfaction scores. If you find significant deviations or trends in the data, it might clue you in to a cultural issue early on. Employee exit interviews will of course be a good source of intel on a problem area (or manager).

Management team meetings. Add the topic of culture friction to the standing agenda of your management team. At least once per quarter, management teams should be focused on how culture might be getting in the way of results, and then design (or delegate to others to design) some plays that will shift the culture. By the way, this might already be happening as a standing agenda item for discussing "risks" in your project management meetings - a lot of culture problems show up in other places without being named as such. **Risks to a project, such as regularly missed deadlines or going over budget and pissing off the client, are perfect examples of the "drag" we mentioned at the beginning of this book, that are the result of one or more of the eight Culture Patterns appearing in your culture.**

Change Management

This one is a bit meta, because it's about designing culture plays that support the running of all the other culture plays. The culture change must be managed, and that is going to take some effort. Here are some plays you might consider.

Develop a culture change roadmap. We apply the Verne Harnish method of strategic line of sight (mentioned in Chapter 4) to culture change work. You should be able to identify your three-year priorities, annual focus areas, and quarterly goals for your culture work just like you do for your regular work.

Activate your change champions. Consider creating an internal culture team drawn from multiple levels in the hierarchy and multiple departments, to assist with all of the culture management activities. This is particularly helpful in supporting grass-roots, bottom-up culture change efforts. NOTE: While we like broad representation on these teams, the most important criteria is enthusiasm for the culture work. Don't require representation from a department if no one there is excited about this work—whoever you get will only annoy you and slow you down.

Train your people in culture change. Get the power to change culture into as many hands as possible.

And if you're not in charge and can't make any of these things happen without approval? Do it guerrilla-style. Make it about getting together socially once a month, for example, and since you're likely to gripe about some culture stuff that is bothering you with your friends anyway, give those group lunches an agenda for coming up with some below-the-radar culture plays you can make happen without approval.

Metrics

Many leaders get busy doing culture change and end up losing sight of the importance of actually measuring progress. Remember, the only reason you are managing your culture is because it can make the organization and the people in it more successful, so you'll need to be intentional about measuring both the progress of the culture change and the impact that change has on results.

The easiest metric to track is the completion or progress of the plays themselves, but in the end, that's not too useful. You should track their progress in your culture change roadmap simply so they don't fall between the cracks and become overlooked. But tracking the number of plays completed (or even which ones were completed) is not as helpful as measuring how people's behavior is changing inside the culture. Quick pulse surveys to staff about how often they are experiencing the behaviors that you wanted to develop in the first place should be your initial metric target. Want to encourage more collaboration between groups? Track how many new projects involve multiple departments and how well they are going in comparison to before.

Don't Overthink It: Just Run Some Plays

Okay, let's take a breath. We know we just gave you a lot there.

There are six categories of plays, some of which are about the ongoing management of the culture change itself—it can feel overwhelming. Don't let that trip you up. The reason it is a lot is because your culture touches every corner of your organization. As we said, you are not going to make a single change and then expect your culture to be transformed, but remember, you don't have to do it all at once either.

The model we gave you is just a structure for organizing the work.

If you're ready to start changing your culture, go back to the four chapters on the patterns. That's where the culture change journey starts: figuring out what patterns are messing with your success.

In the first chapter, we told you how to approach this, so we're going to repeat it here:

> *Once you recognize a Culture Pattern existing in your own organization, it should become VERY EASY to come up with a bunch of ideas for how to fix it. We include some questions to ask yourself about your own business to prompt some brainstorming, and if you need more ideas, head over to culturechangemadeeasybook.com to browse for more. (And hey, if you have already solved for this particular Culture Pattern, please submit your culture plays to benefit others!). We also created some companion resources there. Go check them out when you have a moment.*

Work through each of the Culture Patterns in the same way.

1. *Identify where the Culture Pattern exists in your organization.*
2. *Brainstorm some ways to address it (culture plays).*
3. *Put them into action and change your culture.*

Badabing badaboom!

Just run some plays. Anyone can run a play, even if it just impacts their immediate team. If you want to be more systematic about it, then take a look at the next chapter where we lay out the basics of culture management, with specific advice for different audiences inside your organization, like human resources or the c-suite.

Always have a bias toward action. No team sits out the first half of the game because they are still trying to figure out which play is going to be most successful. They run the plays they have, and then learn from them and adjust.

The same is true for culture change, so let's get started.

If you were reading the Awkward Collaboration chapter before you took a break to read this one, please feel free to go back now to Chapter 3 and continue on with the other three Culture Patterns.

Step 1 is to identify whether you have one of our four main Culture Patterns in your workplace culture.

If you've already read Chapters 1-5, you should feel ready to move forward, but in our final chapter we'll show you how to do this from the top down and from the bottom up—at the same time.

CHAPTER 7

Making the Change Happen

BOTTOM LINE

We've given you tools and frameworks to start changing culture right away. Where you start depends on where you sit in the organization. You'll either be doing culture change from the top down, if you're a senior leader in your organization, or from the bottom up, if you're not.

Either way, let's up our game.

Top down: If you're at the top of an organization (or if you are leading the HR function), then you should focus on professionalizing the function of culture management. This includes putting culture work into job descriptions, building out processes for tracking and managing the change, developing a culture budget, and measuring the ROI of the culture work.

- For the C-Suite specifically, you should focus on investing in culture management, over-communicating the culture, and consciously modeling the behaviors you want to see in your culture.

Bottom up: If you're not in charge, you can still change the culture in your part of the organization. Focus on changing the culture of your own team, and drill down to changing your behaviors. You don't have to be in charge to start creating a better culture, but take an experimental approach that generates results quickly, because you might encounter resistance. We encourage you to embrace AI as a starting point, because it can help you identify culture patterns and competing commitments even if your organization didn't invest in an assessment.

- For middle management specifically, focus on identifying areas of culture friction, because your vantage point is perfect for doing that. Then act as a convenor, bringing together people above you and below you in the hierarchy to start talking through the culture change.

The organizations that change their culture the fastest will win. We wrote this book to make that easier for you, wherever you sit in your organization. So let's get going.

The Best Time to Change Your Culture Is Now

We are biased toward action.

Everything in this book is designed to be applied in the real world.

We want people to work with this book, not just read it.

That's why we broke down the four big Culture Patterns (Awkward Collaboration, Lagging Transparency, Heavy Agility, and Incomplete Innovation), so you could see how they were showing up and causing problems inside organizations. We would bet that many of you read about the patterns, thought of your own organization and said to yourself, "Yeah, that's us."

Then we gave you examples of organizations that have learned how to overcome the pattern, sharing the specific strategies and action items they used to make their cultures stronger, and we gave you a comprehensive playbook model that you can use to design and implement an effective culture change plan. That is culture change made easy. You have everything you need in chapters 1 to 6 to get moving toward a better culture.

Your specific next steps, of course, will depend on where you sit in your organization. There are two directions for culture change, top-down and bottom-up, and both are equally important. It's not about which method you should apply, it's about applying both of them skillfully.

And for both directions, it is time to up our game.

Top-Down: Professionalizing Culture Management

A lot of organizations ignore their culture, for months at a time. We spoke to one HR leader whose organization was acquiring another large firm, and all the work that went into the due diligence, communication efforts, and programs to integrate the new staff into the organization was taxing, particularly for HR. As a result, the people who had been leading the culture change ended up putting zero effort into managing the change for about six months. There just wasn't enough bandwidth.

Our response: Okay, but did you manage your finances during those six months?

No leader would ever tell you that they were ignoring financial management for six months simply because they were too busy. No reconciliations. No checking balances. There's probably enough money in the bank to cover payroll, so we should be fine. No, it doesn't happen that way. Sure, some tasks might fall behind when the finance people get slammed with the M&A work, but the work doesn't just stop, because finance is a core business function. It's not optional.

Yet it's still optional when it comes to culture. Why? Because the finance function has been professionalized, and the culture function has not. **The finance function has a budget, head count, and standardized roles, processes, and systems. If you're serious about culture (which seems likely, if you got this far in this book), then part of your work will be to professionalize your culture management so it matches what the other functions have**.

We referenced our culture management maturity model in the previous chapter (and, again, the full paper is in Appendix D). The model has three stages, and it is in the second stage (culture as a practice) where culture management gets professionalized—where culture design happens and it's where the culture management infrastructure gets built. We assume that most of our readers are either in or entering that second stage. If that's you, and you are in the C-suite or in HR, then make sure you are actively building out the management infrastructure for your culture work, rather than only focusing on the culture change itself. Here are some areas that may need your focus.

People

Your first task is to figure out who is doing the work of culture management. In most organizations, this is going to fall on human resources. We mentioned this briefly in the last chapter in the section on Stewardship plays. Very small organizations may only have 1 or 2 people doing HR, so they will need to rely on the C-suite and other program staff to help with the culture management (this is where having a cross-functional culture team can help). Larger organizations should think about having one or more people with culture specifically in their job titles. These will be the ones to set up and maintain your culture management roadmap, with long-term and short-term goals and priorities. In fact, have them review the section on Stewardship Plays in Chapter 6, because they'll want to stay on top of all of those.

Processes

You'll need a process for staying on top of your culture management activities. In Chapter 4 on Agility, we referenced Verne Harnish's one-page strategic plan, and you should create one of these for your culture management work. We call it a "culture management roadmap," and it includes high-level goals like your core values, but it drills down into 3-5 year priorities, annual focus areas, and then quarterly goals that prioritize which culture plays you will run. The Roadmap should also have a section for tracking culture metrics, such as:

- Employee net promoter score
- Voluntary turnover
- Culture assessment results
- Impact of culture plays on culture
- Impact of culture change on results

Your culture team should be checking in on the roadmap weekly to make sure the quarterly goals remain on track, and every three months you should re-prioritize the culture work based on progress made (or not made) in the previous three months.

Culture Budget

A professionally managed culture has expenses associated with it. The "people" we mentioned above have salaries, for example. Diagnosis, change management, and metrics don't just happen by themselves, so you're going to be spending salary dollars on this. There is no one-size-fits-all approach for determining culture budget and culture headcount, but if you get much above 500 employees, you should probably have at least one of your

HR team devoted primarily to culture management. For smaller organizations, you'll be sharing the culture management functions among your HR team, or, in the case of very small organizations, among staff in various departments. Don't forget, there are also hard costs associated with things like employee surveys and consulting support.

Perhaps more importantly, you'll also need a budget for many of the plays that are developed in the other categories. In some cases, the plays only involve shifting workload so there won't be any additional hard costs (e.g., having a team redesign a particular process to reinforce a new cultural value), but others will require a cash investment, like rolling out a new technology solution or providing training for employees. The line isn't always clear where a culture budget stops and a professional development or IT budget starts (for training and technology solutions, for example), but recognize that those other budgets already feel stretched, so don't limit yourself to "finding" money in those budgets.

In 2019, HBR estimated that companies spend an average of $2,200 per employee, though we assume there is a large variation in that ratio depending on staff size. Following this formula, a small organization like AAE, the case study from Chapter 2, should budget about $60,000 annually, and given what they spent on their culture assessment, consulting support, multiple training programs for staff, and the rollout of new software, that sounds fairly accurate. Larger organizations would likely be well below that per-employee spend of $2,200, but given the potential returns of reducing drag when revenue is in the hundreds of millions or billions, spending hundreds of thousands or even millions on effectively managing culture can be a good investment.

Okay, okay, that might sound like a lot to some folks reading this… but a company that you love working for and look forward to giving your all to?

Priceless, right?

Return On Investment

We might agree, but the finance people may not be convinced. They want to know the literal return on investment, so part of professionalizing culture management is getting disciplined about the ROI of culture change. When you Google "ROI of culture," you'll find a huge range of conclusions, from a 1992 study claiming culture drove a 756% growth in income over an 11 year period, to others that conclude it doesn't exist, or that it's impossible to calculate.

We fall somewhere in the middle. We don't think you'll be able to demonstrate mathematically that culture alone drove a 756% growth in revenue, but we do think you can make some clear and measurable connections between culture and improved results.

As we stated in Chapter 1, Culture Patterns create drag, which comes in the form of things like:

- higher turnover,
- lower engagement,
- more conflict,
- less productivity,
- missed opportunities,
- frustrated customers,
- poor decisions,
- lower quality,
- unnecessary delays, and
- wasted effort.

All that adds up, both in hard costs and opportunity costs. In other words, unless your culture is 100% perfect and not causing any drag, the results you are getting today are lower than they could be. We talked with one CEO who managed some culture change designed specifically to change the way their employees handle conflict and difficult conversations. Months later, when the organization got hit with three very large and complicated projects all at the same time, the CEO noted that all three projects finished ahead of schedule and under budget, a result that he believed would have been unachievable without the culture change. That's what it looks like when you reduce drag. **Investing in culture change produces returns in three main areas: time, quality, and reduced costs.**

Time. Effective culture change almost always results in people making more effective use of their time. Providing information proactively (Lagging

Transparency) and being able to fix things and stop things (Heavy Agility) clearly would save time internally. With that time freed up, employees are able to work on higher-value projects and more effectively reach their strategic objectives. The time-saving impacts HR particularly: think of the time saved when your HR staff don't have to continuously recruit for and onboard the same positions over and over again once turnover rates go down.

Quality. More effective cultures consistently produce higher quality output. The drag produced by the Culture Pattern of Awkward Collaboration, for instance, has a big impact on quality, because the people who should be making contributions aren't, because of the ineffective group collaboration. In addition, fixing the Lagging Transparency pattern tends to result in more effective decision-making, since people are equipped with the right information at the right time.

Reduced costs. Both saving time and improving quality can generate cost savings. Time, as they say, is money, and improved quality means fewer errors that need to be fixed or re-done, and that can save you real dollars. Fixing the pattern of Heavy Agility means you won't be wasting money on programs that are no longer delivering value, and if you can fix your innovation patterns so that innovation is no longer happening in stovepipes, then you'll save costs by not duplicating efforts.

The challenge here is that before you improve your culture, you often don't see the problems that a better culture will solve. Your organization seems to be working fine, and you accept a certain amount of costs or wasted time or lower quality as "the way it is." That's why we use the concept of drag. That sailboat is moving smoothly through the water, and you don't realize that the barnacles on the hull are slowing it down.

We believe most cultures are suffering from a "culture tax" because of the drag they are experiencing. The results you are getting today do not represent your full potential—it's your full potential minus the culture tax, which can be a large percentage if your culture is seriously misaligned.

The sooner you can start calculating what that tax is or might be, the better. It may not be a precise, mathematical calculation, but you should at least try to build a model. Come up with some rough numbers of the costs that could be saved by reducing turnover. Look at specific parts of your operations that are giving you the most trouble and estimate what kind of top-line revenue growth could be achieved by more effective work from your people. Then when you do your culture change, look for the differences. As we said above, you may not be able to show a 100% causal relationship between the culture change and the business results but get as close as you can. The stronger your ROI model is, the easier it will be when you're pitching your leaders to spend money on the culture plays. **Culture is a tangible business tool—start using it like one.**

The Role of the C-Suite

For top-down culture management to be effective, the C-suite needs to up its game. The C-suite must invest in culture management for it to be effective, of course, but there are two other critical areas that can make or break your culture change work: communication and behavior.

There is a great book by Art Kleiner titled *Who Really Matters,* where he argues that people in organizations frequently make up their own minds about what the senior leaders want, and they will move in that direction, even if they are completely wrong about what the senior leaders really want (and trust us, they are frequently wrong). It's a good reminder that even though you may think that you've communicated where you want your culture to go, your people may have come to a different conclusion, so you probably need to communicate it again.

People need to know that the top cares about culture and values the effort that goes into shaping and sustaining a strong culture. Make sure enough of your communications out to staff include key culture messaging, so there is no confusion about what direction you want to go. When you think you may have communicated it enough—communicate it a little more.

The other area that requires the C-suite's attention is their behavior. We talked about this in our definition of culture in Chapter 1. If the behaviors are inconsistent with the words, the behaviors win. Nowhere is this more important than in the C-suite. **You must focus on your behavior and hold each other accountable when the behaviors are not consistent with what**

you want your culture to value. Take a hard look at the way the C-suite might be inadvertently strengthening the Culture Patterns that are getting in the way.

Bottom-Up: Democratizing Culture Change

The more professional culture management that we just talked about is a top-down approach. There is immense value in a systematic approach to managing culture, and we are predicting that more and more organizations will be doing that moving forward. But we've been writing about culture for more than ten years, and while we have covered culture from several different angles, one theme has always been present: the decentralization of power.

Throughout this book, you've seen several quotes and references to our first two books, *Humanize* and *When Millennials Take Over*. Those two plus this book combine to reveal a single narrative, stretched over thirteen years, about the revolution in leadership and management that we have been experiencing. **We are moving away from traditional management of the 20th century, and we are embracing the future of work. The Culture Patterns in our aggregate data show us that we are making progress, but we're not quite there.**

Our books, however, are not only about the future of work. They also identify an overarching trend where power is becoming decentralized. The social internet revolutionized our world by putting power into the hands of the people to create, entertain, inform, and connect, without necessarily requiring a centralized institution. The Millennial generation—shaped by that internet revolution—came into the workforce expecting to wield more power and has been receptive to a more futurist evolution in the workplace.

Now it's time for that decentralization trend to hit culture change. **At the same time that culture management is being professionalized, we believe employees at all levels will start finding opportunities to change,**

nurture, and manage culture on their own. The two ideas are not incompatible—it can be top-down and bottom-up at the same time. In fact, it is more effective that way. It's time to find your power. Here are some ways you can do that.

Embrace Generative Artificial Intelligence

As this book is going to print, the jury is still out on the impact AI is going to have on our world. While not a new thing, AI has leapt to the forefront of just about everything in 2023, because people could see—and experiment with—the power of generative AI. As in previous revolutions, this big change has created a heated debate that quickly devolved into good versus evil. AI is depicted as either a savior that will transform society, or a disaster that will lead to the downfall of humanity. Either is possible, of course, but we think the debate misses a key point: whatever happens, AI is going to put power into the hands of people in the process. When everyone has multiple AI assistants, they suddenly have a lot more power than they used to.

So think about how you can apply this newfound power to culture change. We met with a CIO of a large organization recently who said he wanted to get as many employees as possible using AI in their jobs, not because it would completely revolutionize their work right now, but because it would prepare them for eighteen months from now when the truly revolutionary technology emerges.

The same lesson applies to culture change. Start learning how to use ChatGPT (or its alternatives) so you can use it to help you design culture plays to improve things. Use it as a thinking partner to brainstorm plays, ask it for examples of culture friction you might be missing: literally, ask ChatGPT "what are some examples of workplace culture friction related to [transparency and information sharing / internal collaboration / agility and decision making / innovation]?". Share your own analysis with an AI tool and ask it to suggest improvements or ask it what you might be missing. Remember what the CIO said—the real revolution probably isn't here yet, but the more skill you have in working with these tools, the more quickly you will be able to leverage the more powerful ones to enable culture change from the ground up.

Change the Culture of Your Team

You don't have to change the entire culture of your organization to see results—you can start with your own team. Go back to the chapters on the Culture Patterns and think about how they apply at a team level. For example, the lagging transparency pattern is about being reactive rather than proactive. The examples of culture plays we gave you included big things like changing the company onboarding process or rolling out a new intranet. Think about what the equivalents would be for your individual team. Here are some examples:

- You could share your own internal team-level KPIs with each other and create a team dashboard.
- You could create a channel on Slack where team members could make daily updates on what they have been working on.
- You could "flip" your internal team meetings, where individual reports are sent ahead of time and the meeting time itself is devoted to problem-solving and decision-making.

Incorporate culture conversations into your team-building activities. Develop a set of culture priorities for your own team, even if they are slightly different from the culture priorities your organization is focused on (and especially if your company is not focused on culture at all!). Then drill down to the specific behaviors that your team needs to value to move forward with the culture change.

If you skipped the top-down section, make sure to go back and read the section on ROI. This applies to the work you can do on your own team as well. Build an ROI model focusing only on your team's projects. It could come in handy if you need any money to run your plays.

Change Your Own Behavior

You can even bring culture change down into the realm of your individual behavior, because, in the end, that's all you really control anyway. This may not have a massive impact on the overall culture, but every little bit helps. Again, apply the ROI thinking to you as an individual. Come up with a model about how much more effective your own work would be if you could do things like being more proactive in your communication or collaborating more effectively with colleagues in other departments. Then test it out and see if you can put some concrete value on the results. If you see some real improvement, then try sharing it with colleagues, and perhaps you can build some momentum for some larger change.

But even if you can't build momentum, don't stop making changes in your own world and improving things. Be the change you want to see.

Change from the Middle

In addition to the advice above, we wanted to give some specific tips for middle managers. We noticed that in many culture assessments that we ran, middle management reported more traditional scores than both senior leaders and individual contributors. In other words, middle management tends to experience the culture as less transparent, less agile, less collaborative, and less innovative than nearly everyone else in the organization. There are systemic reasons for this.

In Chapter 2 we talked about Barry Oshry's book, *Seeing Systems*, and what he called the "dance of the blind reflex." In every system, the different parts of the system (top, middle, bottom) fall into traditional patterns that tend to make each of them unhappy. For the middles, it's about being torn: trying to serve the needs of both the tops and the bottoms at the same time.

Instead of being torn between the two ends of the ladder, try to leverage your unique position in two ways to support culture change:

- **Spot the culture friction.** You have visibility into the worlds of both the tops and the bottoms. Instead of being frustrated that you can't see everything, use that perspective to spot areas of culture friction. You might be able to name them faster than the other two groups.
- **Be a convenor.** Instead of trying to fix the problems yourself (you'll end up feeling torn again), get the right people in the room

and have them figure out how to redesign that problematic process that is causing the culture friction. You need to connect the right people, give them the right tools, and then let them do their thing.

Be Ready for Resistance

"Proceed Until Apprehended" was the title of the last chapter of *When Millennials Take Over.* That was the mantra of Florence Nightingale, a nurse who essentially invented the modern hospital in the 19th century. In her context, as a woman, specifically, she didn't have the luxury of asking for permission to do things in new ways. She had to just do it, knowing that someone above her would eventually discover her deviant behavior and "apprehend" her, pointing out that her new method or approach was not sanctioned.

That is your organization's "immune system" springing into action. Every organization has one, where people consistently intervene as soon as they realize something is being done in a way that was not expected or different from tradition. You'll never get rid of this immune system, so learn how to work with it.

The trick is to design your culture change (even if it's only for your team) as rapid experiments. When you make those unilateral moves to change culture (like changing your team meetings or using a new Slack channel) be sure to identify the results you got from making these changes as quickly as you can. You're not just doing things in a new way, you're doing things that will intentionally generate better results.

That way, when the immune system does apprehend you (and it will), you can show it the results you got. Immune systems are not convinced by "I thought this would be a good idea," but they are often swayed by "Yes, but look at the good results I got."

Whoever Changes Culture the Fastest Wins

In Chapter 2 we told the story of AAE, the nonprofit that overcame the Culture Pattern of Awkward Collaboration by reducing cognitive load and making hierarchy more accessible. What we didn't tell you, however, is that they implemented the bulk of that change during the pandemic.

They had prioritized their culture change efforts literally the week before the country went on lockdown in March 2020. Like everyone else, they had to stop and make some huge adjustments in a short period of time. That meant putting the culture work on hold for a few months as they put out the fires and righted the ship. Everybody did that in the spring of 2020. But by May, they were up and running again with the culture work. They did some re-prioritizing, given all that had changed, but then got straight to work running their culture plays and making changes.

Another organization we worked with was in a similar position. They started implementing their culture change at the very end of 2019, and they, too, had to put it on hold in 2020, but, unfortunately, they never really got back to it. That decision certainly felt justified—there was simply too much going on and too much changing, so they just couldn't devote time to doing the culture change work.

Two years later, both organizations gathered some new culture data, which included the employee Net Promoter Score (eNPS), which is a key measure of employee engagement. This metric was included in the culture assessment that they both ran in 2019, so they were looking to see improvement. The eNPS ranges between -100 and +100, and the average is about a +20. AAE scored quite high when they first took their assessment, at a +40. The other organization was slightly below average with a +5.

When they measured again, however, AAE—who had consistently worked to improve their culture despite adapting to the pandemic—had risen to a very impressive +50, while the other organization dropped 25 points to a -20. Interestingly, the rest of that organization's culture data didn't show much change. They were about as traditional in 2022 as they were in 2020 and the patterns hadn't changed, but their inability to implement the change damaged employee engagement seriously.

This is what we mean by "whoever changes the culture fastest, wins." This is why we believe leaders should strengthen their culture management function, and individuals should start changing their behavior both individually and within their teams. This is why we argue that culture management should be professionalized. This is why seeing your Culture Patterns is so important.

You have some choices to make. You must choose what approach you will take to managing your culture. You must choose how to engage with the work of culture change. We hope that the tools and concepts we shared in this book will make your choices—and the work you do after making those choices—easier, because we believe the work of culture is going to become exponentially more important in the years to come.

Let's get to it.

Appendices

APPENDIX A:

THE EIGHT CULTURE PATTERNS

In this book we did a deep dive into the four culture patterns of Awkward Collaboration, Lagging Transparency, Heavy Agility, and Incomplete Innovation. In our research, however, we have identified 8 primary Culture Patterns, one for each of the 8 Culture Markers that we measure in our culture assessment.

The four remaining patterns are:
- Micro Inclusion
- Intangible Growth
- Shallow Solutions
- Incrementally Digital (Technologies)

Here is a brief summary of all 8 patterns (listed alphabetically, by Culture Marker) for your reference.

Heavy Agility

VALUE IMBALANCE:	Valuing **forward action** more than **effective action**.
COMPETING COMMITMENT:	Commitment to **progress and speed** is neutralized by a commitment to **novelty and creation**.
DATA PATTERN:	**3.66** Forward action **3.38** Effective action

Organizations with this pattern value forward action more than they value effective action. In other words, they are making great efforts to maintain speed without losing quality and they embrace change, yet there is not enough attention put toward fixing things that are broken or stopping activities that no longer add value.

These organizations have a strong commitment to progress and speed that is neutralized by a stronger commitment to novelty and creation. These organizations genuinely want agility, but aren't doing the blocking and tackling required to make it happen, and as a result, they miss opportunities, frustrate their employees and leave money on the table. In that sense, they are achieving agility without having shed some of the weight that was slowing them down to begin with, hence the term "heavy agility." They are trying to push decision making down, but the senior level is not quite getting out of the way. And their inability to consistently fix things or stop things when needed is also holding them back.

Organizations that have overcome this pattern have learning deeply embedded in their culture, which includes a disciplined approach to using data and a commitment to co-creating value with customers and stakeholders, both internally and externally.

Awkward Collaboration

VALUE IMBALANCE:	Valuing **collaborative individuals** more than **collaborative groups.**
COMPETING COMMITMENT:	Commitment to **working together** is neutralized by a commitment to the **autonomy of subgroups**.
DATA PATTERN:	**4.12** Collaborative individuals **3.49** Collaborative groups

Organizations with this pattern value collaborative individuals more than they value collaborative groups. In other words, they're creating cultures where people are very willing to help each other out, but it's mostly person-to-person, and they are not emphasizing how whole departments or different levels of the hierarchy should be collaborating more effectively.

Their commitment to collaboration is neutralized by a commitment to the autonomy of subgroups, so they care about collaboration, and people collaborate all the time—it's just awkward and less effective than it could be. They are trying to involve people from other departments, but they are often too late. They're missing out on opportunities to learn from what our colleagues are doing. They end up picking and choosing when they define collaboration as essential, and when they define it as interference.

Organizations that have overcome this pattern make it easier for groups to collaborate by clarifying and simplifying processes in ways that reduce the cognitive load among employees, and they find ways to make their hierarchies more accessible.

Intangible Growth

VALUE IMBALANCE:	Valuing **aspirational growth** more than **developmental growth**.
COMPETING COMMITMENT:	Commitment to **reaching the next level** is neutralized by a commitment to **standardized solutions**.
DATA PATTERN:	**4.02** Aspirational growth **3.55** Developmental growth

Organizations with this pattern value aspirational growth more than they value developmental growth. In other words, they have a commitment to creating organizations that support people's passions and communities, but they focus less on the health, welfare, and development of those unique employees.

These organizations have a commitment to reaching the next level that is neutralized by a commitment to standardized solutions. In that sense, they have become more about addressing higher level concepts of growth than valuing the individual needs of their people—it's still growth, but it's less tangible for people. This makes real employee engagement very difficult, because the aspirational ideals end up being thwarted when the employees feel like they can't be successful at a deeply personal level.

Organizations that have overcome this pattern have learned how to integrate systems thinking into their operations, allowing them to build capacity continuously, and embrace autonomy at all levels of the system.

Micro Inclusion

VALUE IMBALANCE:	Valuing **personal inclusion** more than **structural inclusion.**
COMPETING COMMITMENT:	Commitment to **including difference** is neutralized by a commitment to **earned authority.**
DATA PATTERN:	**4.23** Personal inclusion **3.69** Structural inclusion

Organizations with this pattern value personal inclusion more than they value structural inclusion. In other words, they support people in being authentic and comfortable around each other as people, but they have yet to figure out how to include most of them in planning or strategic thinking.

These organizations have a commitment to including difference that is neutralized by a commitment to earned authority. Privileges associated with rising through the ranks are maintained. In that sense, they have narrowed their inclusion focus, ensuring that individuals feel personally included, without necessarily including them at a strategic level—micro inclusion. This creates some positive personal sentiment but fails to fully leverage the power of diversity inside the organization.

Organizations that have overcome this pattern shift their perspective from "power over" to "power with." They are closer to unlocking the true potential of the humans inside their organization, because they are intentionally reducing the barriers to everyone's full participation in the system.

Incomplete Innovation

VALUE IMBALANCE:	Valuing **innovation concepts** more than **innovation practices.**
COMPETING COMMITMENT:	Commitment to **creating new value** is neutralized by a commitment to **appearing competent and being right.**
DATA PATTERN:	**3.88** Reactive transparency **3.46** Proactive transparency

Organizations with this pattern value the concepts of innovation more than they value the practices of innovation. In other words, they are asking people to be creative and future focused, even to "hack" existing processes, but they are farther behind when it comes to taking real risks, running experiments, or beta testing products or services.

These organizations have a commitment to creating new value that is neutralized by a stronger commitment to appearing competent providing the right answers. These organizations genuinely want innovation, but they are afraid to do what it takes, and as a result, they fail to capture new value and lose ground on their competition.

Organizations that have overcome this pattern have built the capacity to manage change into every level of the organization and intentionally create a culture of psychological safety. They also ensure that collaboration includes opportunities for cross-pollination among groups.

Shallow Solutions

VALUE IMBALANCE:	Valuing **solving problems** more than **meeting needs.**
COMPETING COMMITMENT:	Commitment to **serving people** is neutralized by a commitment to **personal responsibility.**
DATA PATTERN:	**3.87** Solving problems **3.42** Meeting needs

Organizations with this pattern value solving problems more than they value meeting needs. In other words, they obviously care about solving customer problems, and they might be flexible with surface level benefits for employees, but they fall short of designing solutions based on the needs and unique situations of both employees and customers.

These organizations have a commitment to serving people (internally and externally) that is neutralized by a commitment to personal responsibility. Deeper needs are considered the responsibility of the individuals, not the organization, and that leads to a focus on the issues that present themselves most obviously, rather than addressing the underlying drivers—shallow solutions. This typically results in slow growth and the inefficiency of duplicated effort, as the same problem must be solved repeatedly until the deeper issues are handled.

Organizations that have overcome this pattern have built a sense of shared responsibility at every level. This allows for more flexibility and an emphasis on long-term gains rather than just short-term.

Incrementally Digital (Technologies)

VALUE IMBALANCE:	Valuing **digital mindsets** more than **digital tools.**
COMPETING COMMITMENT:	Commitment to **digital transformation** is neutralized by a commitment to a **return on existing investments.**
DATA PATTERN:	**3.76** Digital mindsets **3.45** Digital tools

Organizations with this pattern value digital mindsets more than they value digital tools. In other words, they are emphasizing digital concepts like quick access to resources and a focus on user experience, but they are holding back on an investment in technology that achieves levels of reliability and functionality that would unlock true digital transformation.

These organizations have a commitment to digital transformation that is neutralized by a commitment to getting a return on solutions they have already invested in. They settle for the journey being more incremental than transformative. They give their people enough tech and resources to make some progress, but not necessarily enough. As a result, employees are often frustrated, as they see the potential of digital transformation, but do not have access to the tools or resources they need to achieve it.

Organizations that have overcome this pattern have decided to stop being penny wise and pound foolish and invest in true digital transformation. If our tight technology budgets make us do more with less, then we will be missing out on the potentially huge returns of a smart digital transformation strategy.

Lagging Transparency

VALUE IMBALANCE:	Valuing **reactive transparency** more than **proactive transparency.**
COMPETING COMMITMENT:	Commitment to **sharing information** is neutralized by a commitment to **controlling information**.
DATA PATTERN:	**3.83** Reactive transparency **3.38** Proactive transparency

Organizations with this pattern value reactive transparency more than they value proactive transparency. In other words, if individuals ask someone for information, they are happy to share it, but these organizations don't put in systems and processes to make sure that information is already in people's hands before they even thought of asking for it.

These organizations have a commitment to information sharing that is neutralized by a competing commitment to maintaining control over the information, so they care about transparency, but it happens both too little and too late. They force themselves to make decisions based on incomplete or even inaccurate information.

Organizations that have overcome this pattern are disciplined in how they build and maintain a transparency architecture, using both technology and processes. is. They also embrace the responsibility that goes along with greater transparency to meeting employee needs and solving problems for them.

APPENDIX B:
THE DATA

For each of the four Culture Patterns that we covered in Chapters 2-5, we broke the pattern down, sharing some of the data from our culture assessment's aggregate data set. For those of you who like the numbers, we created this appendix so you can see all of the data we shared in those chapters in one place.

Below there are eight tables: two for each Culture Pattern, since the patterns all are based on a competing commitment where part of the marker is valued more and is more present than another part. Each pattern component has three individual building blocks in it, so we share those scores and show you where they rank among all 64 building blocks measured in the assessment (with 1 being the highest scoring and 64 the lowest).

We also provide a correlation coefficient that identifies the strength of the correlation with each Building Block to the last question that is asked in the assessment: "How likely are you to recommend someone you respect to work here?" Answers are on a 0 to 10 scale, and we use the Net Promoter Score methodology to come up with a single employee net promoter score (eNPS).

We believe the eNPS is a good measure of employee engagement, so we think it's significant to note which Building Blocks had stronger or weaker correlations with that question. All the Blocks in the survey have a positive correlation with the eNPS question, with coefficients ranging between 0.26 and 0.61. A coefficient above 0.7 is considered "strong" and below 0.3 is considered "weak." The median correlation coefficient in our data set is 0.50

Awkward Collaboration:

Collaborative Individuals

Building Block:	Avg.	Rank	Correlation to eNPS
Collaborative Individuals (pattern component)	4.12	2/16	0.48
Sharing the workload (block)	4.37	1/64	0.42
Leveraging relationships (block)	4.02	10/64	0.51
Facilitation (block)	3.97	11/64	0.50

Sharing the Workload had the highest score of all 64 Building Blocks, but it's correlation with eNPS was not as strong as the other Blocks in this pattern component.

Collaborative Groups

Building Block:	Avg.	Rank	Correlation to eNPS
Collaborative groups (pattern component)	3.49	11/16	0.47
Cross-functional communications (block)	3.32	61/64	0.48
Boundaries, Borders & Territories (block)	3.39	54/64	0.47
Communication Platforms (block)	3.75	24/64	0.47

The eNPS correlations for all three Blocks are below the median.

Lagging Transparency:

Reactive Transparency

Building Block:	Avg.	Rank	Correlation to eNPS
Collaborative Individuals (pattern component)	3.83	6/16	0.54
Sharing the workload (block)	4.04	8/64	0.57
Leveraging relationships (block)	3.77	21/64	0.57
Facilitation (block)	3.68	31/64	0.49

The entire Marker of Transparency (made up of 8 Building Blocks) has a 0.51 correlation with the Marker of Agility in the aggregate data set, which is the strongest of any two Markers.

Proactive Transparency

Building Block:	Avg.	Rank	Correlation to eNPS
Collaborative Individuals (pattern component)	3.38	15/16	0.47
Sharing the workload (block)	3.46	51/64	0.50
Leveraging relationships (block)	3.34	59/64	0.54
Facilitation (block)	3.33	60/64	0.36

Hard truths (is the senior level honest about the tough decisions it makes) had one of the lowest scores, but one of the highest eNPS correlations.

Heavy Agility:

Forward Action

Building Block:	Avg.	Rank	Correlation to eNPS
Forward action (pattern component)	3.66	6/16	0.48
Quality management (block)	3.80	8/64	0.42
Managing change (block)	3.62	21/64	0.51
Distribution of power (block)	3.56	31/64	0.50

This component reflects the part of the pattern where we "excel," yet it ranked only 9th out of 16 components.

Effective Action

Building Block:	Avg.	Rank	Correlation to eNPS
Effective action (pattern component)	3.36	6/16	0.49
Leadership facilitation (block)	3.47	49/64	0.50
Efficiency (block)	3.34	58/64	0.49
Changing directions (block)	3.28	63/64	0.48

Agility is the lowest Marker overall, averaging 3.52 (average of all the data is 3.69), and you can see that this component is the lowest scoring of them all as well.

Incomplete Innovation:

Innovation Concepts

Building Block:	Avg.	Rank	Correlation to eNPS
Innovation Concepts (pattern component)	3.88	4/16	0.51
Future focus (block)	3.95	12/64	0.50
Inspiration (block)	3.89	14/64	0.53
Creativity (block)	3.79	20/64	0.52

All of the eNPS correlations are above the median

Innovation Practices

Building Block:	Avg.	Rank	Correlation to eNPS
Innovation practices (pattern component)	3.46	12/16	0.46
Experimentation (block)	3.53	45/64	0.43
Risk taking (block)	3.49	48/64	0.49
Testing new ideas (block)	3.36	56/64	0.44

All of the eNPS correlations are below the median.

More Data Points From The Aggregate Data Set:

Overall Average	3.69	
Data points	1,228,240	
eNPS Median	+19	
Most Futurist Marker	3.92	Inclusion
Least Futurist Marker:	3.52	Agility
Most Futurist Blocks:	4.37	Sharing the workload
	4.28	Acceptance
	4.27	Passion and purpose
	4.22	Diversity
	4.18	Customer influence
Least Futurist Blocks:	3.16	People-centric solutions
	3.28	Changing directions
	3.31	Incorporating outside perspectives
	3.32	Cross-functional communication
	3.33	Information availability
Top Marker Correlations:	0.514	Agility and Transparency
	0.503	Growth and Innovation
	0.488	Agility and Collaboration
Top eNPS Correlations:	0.615	Health and Welfare
	0.613	Tailored Responses
	0.572	Ownership
	0.568	Information Credibility
	0.565	Trust
Bottom eNPS Correlations:	0.261	Customer Influence
	0.299	Customized Engagement
	0.342	Flexibility
	0.359	Information Availability
	0.379	Reliable Technology

If you'd like to learn more about the assessment, visit https://propelnow.co/culture-assessment/

APPENDIX C:
THE RACI MODEL

We are including this culture play as an appendix because it's one of the resources most requested by our clients, and Googling "RACI model" is unsatisfactory at best, as there are a variety of definitions and explanations. Here is ours.

Many organizations assume that their organizational chart is enough for everyone to understand decision-making authority. However, this is not always the case, particularly within collaborating groups. To address this, there is a model called RACI (Responsible, Accountable, Consulted, and Informed) that defines decision-making roles with specific responsibilities and expectations. While there are various interpretations of RACI, disciplined application of the model can be very effective in resolving conflicts arising from unclear decision-making roles. Here is how we define these role categories.

RESPONSIBLE

This is the decision maker, i.e., the person responsible for deciding. This is usually a single person, and this person will always be deeply and actively involved in the project. If you're thinking, "this is MY project," then you're probably the R on most decisions. It is possible to have multiple Rs, though in that case, ALL of the Rs must be in unanimous agreement before making a decision (which can complicate things).

ACCOUNTABLE

This is typically the "boss" of the decision maker—someone who is accountable for the results that will happen (or not happen) depending on the outcome of the decisions made by the R. The A is usually the person who delegated decision-making responsibility to the R. While they do not get into the weeds of the project, an A is regularly updated on progress and technically can exercise veto power over decisions if it's really important. That veto power is the key characteristic of the A role.

CONSULTED

This category is for people who *must* be consulted before a decision is made. You don't need to identify everyone who might be asked a question or provide input on a project, but this is for people who the R knows need to weigh in before the decision is made. It would be a mistake to decide without their input. However it should also be noted that the R still gets to make the decision—you can always say no to input from a C (if you couldn't say no to their input, then they are probably an A).

INFORMED

The last category is for people who should be informed about the decision after it is made. They are relevant enough to need to know what the decision was, but they do not need to be part of the decision-making process. This role doesn't usually cause too many complications unless the people in this category feel they should be either in the A or the C roles. Many senior managers are in this role—they need to know what's happening—but they sometimes slip and feel like they are accountable and can veto just because of their position. Even the CEO can be in the I role. Theoretically, the CEO could be an A on every decision—if the buck stops with them, can't they veto anything? Yes, but is that what you want your CEO to spend time on?

The RACI model is particularly useful in clarifying roles and responsibilities in complex projects or organizational structures. Let's consider a business example involving the development of a new software product at a tech company to illustrate the different roles in the RACI model:

Scenario 1: Development of a New Software Product

1. Responsible (R): Emma, the Lead Software Developer.

    + Emma is in charge of the technical development of the new software product. She makes key decisions about the software architecture, coding standards, and feature implementation. As the primary decision-maker, she's deeply involved in the project's day-to-day activities.

2. Accountable (A): Liam, the Project Manager.

+ Liam is responsible for the overall success of the software project. He has delegated the technical decision-making to Emma, but he is ultimately accountable for the project's outcome. He keeps track of the project's progress and has veto power over decisions, ensuring they align with the broader goals of the project. However, he does not involve himself in the technical minutiae.

3. Consulted (C): Aisha, the User Experience (UX) Designer, and Noah, the Senior Database Architect.

+ Aisha provides critical input on user interface and experience aspects, ensuring the software is user-friendly and meets customer expectations.

+ Noah advises on database design and optimization, ensuring the software's back-end can handle the expected load and data requirements.

+ Both Aisha and Noah are consulted for their expertise, but the final decision rests with Emma.

4. 4. Informed (I): Olivia, the CEO, and other department heads.

+ Olivia and the department heads are kept informed about the progress and major decisions of the software project. They need to be aware of how the project aligns with the company's strategic goals and how it impacts various departments. However, they are not directly involved in the day-to-day decision-making process.

In this example, the RACI model helps to delineate the roles and responsibilities clearly. Emma, as the Responsible, is the primary decision-maker; Liam, the Accountable, oversees the project's success and has veto power; Aisha and Noah, the Consulted, provide essential input; and Olivia, along with other department heads as the Informed, are kept up-to-date on significant developments. This clarity ensures efficient decision-making and accountability, while minimizing conflicts and misunderstandings about roles.

However, let's consider a scenario in a non-profit organization where the decision-making lines are less clear, making the application of the RACI model more challenging:

Scenario 2: Implementation of a New Fundraising Strategy

1. Responsible (R): Alex, the Fundraising Coordinator.

   + Alex is tasked with developing and implementing the new fundraising strategy. While Alex is expected to make day-to-day decisions about the strategy, the lines are blurred because of the need for extensive collaboration and input from various departments.

2. Accountable (A): Jordan, the Director of Development.

   + Jordan, as Alex's superior, is accountable for the overall success of the fundraising strategy. However, Jordan's role becomes muddier as they often delve into the details, offering specific ideas and directions, which sometimes conflict with Alex's decisions. This overlap creates tension and confusion about the final decision-making authority.

3. Consulted (C): Taylor, the Marketing Manager, and Casey, the Community Outreach Lead.

   + Taylor's input on marketing the fundraising campaign is crucial, but their strong opinions often overshadow Alex's decisions, blurring the line between being consulted and taking on a decision-making role.
   + Casey provides essential insights into community engagement, but there's ambiguity about whether their suggestions are just consultative or if they carry an implicit expectation of being implemented, further complicating Alex's decision-making process.

4. Informed (I): Various Department Heads and Board Members.

+ The heads of different departments and board members need to be informed about the fundraising strategy. However, they sometimes overstep their informational role by offering unsolicited advice or expressing concerns, which Alex feels compelled to consider, even though these stakeholders are not part of the decision-making process.

In this example, the RACI model's effectiveness is challenged by overlapping roles and a lack of clear boundaries. Alex, while responsible, faces interference and strong influences from both the Consulted and the Informed groups. Jordan's role as Accountable is muddled by their direct involvement in operational decisions, which should ideally be Alex's domain. The Consulted parties, Taylor and Casey, often act as if they have decision-making authority, while the Informed group, including the board members, indirectly influences decisions beyond just being kept in the loop. This scenario highlights the importance of not only assigning roles clearly but also ensuring that all parties understand and respect the boundaries of their respective roles in the decision-making process.

As a culture play to implement, the RACI model can be an extremely useful tool in your culture toolbox, but all parties need to commit to following it—a perfect example of where you need to look for competing commitments where the change you're trying to make in your culture might face some resistance.

One word of caution: don't get drawn into the weeds when implementing RACI. We've seen organizations try to break down just about every existing task into a RACI chart where all staff are put into one of the boxes. This takes forever, and when you make it that detailed, it loses its meaning. Instead, use it specifically in areas where there is confusion. The shared language and concepts will help smooth the decision-making process without making people jump through unnecessary hoops every time they start a project.

APPENDIX D:
CULTURE MANAGEMENT MATURITY MODEL

In chapter 6 we gave a very brief summary of the culture management maturity model that we developed back in 2019. In this Appendix, we provide the details for leaders who want to improve their culture management maturity.

The model is based on the premise that culture is a business function and should be managed intentionally, just as we do other functions, like finance or IT. Maturity, in this case, is based on how complex and comprehensive you make your approach to the work of culture. There are three basic stages of maturity:

- **Culture as a concept,** which includes organizations that ignore culture altogether, but also ones that focus on ideals and core values.
- **Culture as a practice,** where organizations put effort into designing and then managing culture at the level of processes, structures, and technologies.
- **Culture as a system,** where culture is embedded into structures and even integrated into leadership and strategy.

In the original white paper from 2019, we represented the model graphically, using one of our favorite images from science, art, and nature: a spiral generated by the golden ratio.[1]

---

1 https://www.adobe.com/creativecloud/design/discover/golden-ratio.html

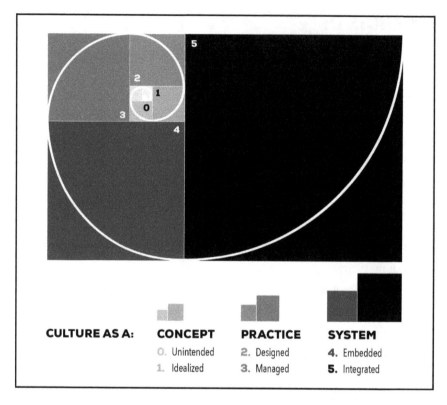

CULTURE AS A:	CONCEPT	PRACTICE	SYSTEM
	0. Unintended	2. Designed	4. Embedded
	1. Idealized	3. Managed	5. Integrated

You can see that each of the three stages has two levels, so the maturity progression is from Level 0 (Unintended) up to Level 5 (Integrated). We chose the spiral image because we believe that progression in the model is not necessarily a straight line. There is likely movement forward and back or returning to perfect lower levels once you've done work at a higher level. But either way, growth is achieved by moving up the spiral. You don't necessarily need to be at level 5 to have a healthy and productive culture, but we have consistently found, in both our practice and research, that the truly exceptional companies—the ones that people literally can't imagine ever wanting to leave—have mastered culture management at the highest levels.

Culture is fundamentally about what is valued inside an organization, and because values are concepts, this is where the culture journey starts. The work of Stage 1 will focus on clarifying and articulating the concepts that describe an organization's ideal culture, though not all organizations have even progressed that far.

Level 0. Unintended

The simplest way to look at culture is as a concept. Culture, as we defined in chapter 1, is about what is valued, and values are obviously concepts. At the lowest level of culture management, however, even the concept of culture is ignored. Instead, leaders are focused exclusively on strategy and operations. A classic example would be a start-up company. In the early days, start-ups are typically focused on securing enough cash to keep the doors open and proving a market for their products or services. In this environment, culture falls victim to a "Maslow's hierarchy" kind of choice: when you're fighting for survival, it's hard to find time or energy to think about what is valued or what kind of principles need to be articulated and supported as part of your culture. Such time is considered a luxury.

Of course, ignoring culture doesn't mean you don't have one. You either have a culture by design or a culture by default, and for start-ups, it's primarily by default. Start-up culture is created by the de facto behaviors and attitudes of the people inside the organization, particularly the founders and other senior leaders because when it comes to defining culture, we tend to look "up" in the hierarchy. If the founder is excessively detail-oriented, for example, then you're likely to have a workplace culture that focuses on details. As an organization grows, you might see a counter-culture develop among staff who push back against the founder's values (particularly when the employees feel it is hindering their success), but you're unlikely to see real culture change unless the senior level agrees to such change.

Just because a culture is unintended, by the way, does not mean that it's always bad. Many default cultures can evolve in ways that are effective and positive. As long as the natural behavior patterns of the founders end up aligning with what makes the company successful, the culture will be a positive one. Where it gets tough is when a company's success drivers change, but the founders are unwilling to adjust their approach.

In the end, however, success generated by unintended culture is similar to success at a roulette wheel: it's just luck. There's nothing wrong with a little luck in business, but it's no foundation upon which to build a truly strong or sustainable culture. This is why Level 0 in our model is termed

"Unintended": you won't be able to identify any developmental progress until you at least pay some conscious attention to your culture, which is precisely what happens in the next level, "Idealized."

Characteristics of an Unintended Culture:
- Cultural ideals are communicated informally and inconsistently.
- No formal processes are in place for defining or improving culture.
- The definition of culture (and any specific culture change) is driven exclusively from the top.

Level 1. Idealized

As soon as you start thinking consciously about what your organization's culture really is—and what you think it should be, you have moved to the next level in our maturity model. "Idealized" is still in Stage 1, so the focus remains on concepts, but now the organization is putting time and effort into defining its ideal culture and then capturing that ideal in some kind of tangible artifact, like a document, slide deck, or wall poster. Organizations at this stage sometimes also invest in tangible perks or annual events that they believe reflect their ideal culture.

Perhaps the most obvious indicator that a company has moved into Level 1 is the existence of some kind of Core Values document. We have a love/hate relationship with core values, but there's no denying their popularity. One recent survey[2] showed that 89% of American companies report having some form of documented corporate core values, which indicates that they're trying to connect the work of their organization to some deeper purpose and meaning. And, because purpose and meaning really matter to human beings, core values can be used to help align internal behaviors and attract the right kind of people.

In practice, however, core values often end up defaulting to generic values that may be agreeable but rarely impact internal behavior or really distinguish your culture from anyone else's. High-level values are separated from everyday

2 https://www.strategy-business.com/article/05206?gko=9c265

behavior and are thus frequently ineffective guides.

A more effective set of core values actually makes an explicit connection between a value and the specific behaviors that represent that value in the real world. Netflix's famous culture slide deck[3] is a good example.

Once the core concepts of a culture become articulated, they must be intentionally shared with employees. This represents the other half of the work at Level 1: creating artifacts and rituals, the symbolic vehicles for communicating culture. The most common artifact within workplace cultures is the documentation of core values via PDF, slide deck, poster, etc. We encourage organizations to hold themselves to a high standard of clarity and precision when developing culture artifacts, which includes being specific about behaviors and explaining why a core value makes both the organization and its employees more successful. Rituals are gatherings, meetings, parties, etc., that communicate and reinforce cultural values. While they can be as simple as parties or other events focused on fun and community, some organizations inject more sophisticated symbols into their rituals to communicate more nuanced aspects of their culture.

Starting with core values and ensuring internal behaviors are aligned with those values is not the only way to create an idealized culture. Some companies choose a more "inside- out" approach by understanding the nuances of employee experience and addressing internal team dynamics as a path to defining culture at the behavioral level. Employee engagement surveys fall into this category, but this could also include administering a personality-type or work-style assessment (e.g., Predictive Index or DiSC) and discussing the results as a group.

By raising awareness of different styles of behavior, they enable team members to work more effectively together. This may also come as a staff retreat or an off-site activity, where conflicts or tough conversations can be intentionally facilitated to work through key performance issues. While these efforts are not necessarily tied to articulated concepts in the culture (which happens

---

3 https://www.slideshare.net/reed2001/culture-1798664

at the next level), they do reflect a level of attention to culture and internal dynamics that warrant inclusion in Level 1.

Level 2. Designed

Moving from Level 1 to Level 2 brings you into a new stage in the model: **culture as a practice, as in taking your ideas and intentionally putting them into practice.** Once your concepts are clearly articulated, you need to bring them into real-world existence, which requires concrete action plans, processes, and organizational support.

Design is about creating a blueprint for converting concepts into reality, in this case, your culture. This book, as you may have noticed, is largely about Level 2 work. Our definition of culture design has four basic steps:

1. Identify your Culture Patterns
2. Discern your organizational success drivers
3. Write up a culture change playbook
4. Set up your culture operations infrastructure.

In Chapters 2-5, we went into great detail about four of the eight Culture Patterns from our research, and in Appendix B we share the basics on the other four as well. We think we made a compelling case for the importance of seeing your Culture Patterns (and the competing commitments inside of them) and identifying how they are currently messing with success.

Culture design is not only about solving existing problems. It should also be about proactively aligning culture with what we call "success drivers." Success drivers are discrete factors, either inside your organization or out in your environment, that have a disproportionate impact on your ability to get the results you want. Your superpowers, if you will. They do not encapsulate every single factor required for an organization to succeed.

Some will be internal—a concept or a process you created that sets you apart or drives productivity. And some will be external—a strategic opportunity for leverage or a new expectation your market has for you at your stage of development. So you don't want "good" Culture Patterns in the abstract— you want Culture Patterns specifically aligned to your organizational success drivers.

With both the starting point and destination clear, you need to start putting one foot in front of the other and will want to assemble a variety of techniques for doing so, and that's what we covered in Chapter 6 when we got into the Culture Change Playbook model.

Start Building Your Culture Operations Infrastructure

One of the key differences between Level 1 and Level 2 is that the latter requires a significant investment of resources in culture work. We started discussing this in Chapter 6 when we covered the "Stewardship" section of your Playbook. Organizations at this level typically do not yet have an annual culture budget but are already spending money to begin the establishment of their Culture Operations infrastructure, i.e., the people and processes that ensure that the work of culture gets done sustainably over time. Investments are typically directed toward staff time (changing job descriptions to give people time to do the ongoing culture work), consultants (to help people with the design process, but also to help build other capacities internally), and play implementation (which can include spending additional time/money on staff and consultants to run the plays, but also investments in technology or training).

Characteristics of a Designed Culture:

- Completion of a qualitative or quantitative culture assessment.
- Specific processes, structures, or technologies are intentionally altered (via plays in a playbook) to align the culture with success.
- Time, money, and other resources are spent improving culture.
- Senior management is visibly committed to intentionally shaping culture.
- The initial infrastructure for your culture operations is in place.

Level 3. Managed

To reach Level 3, you will need to make an important choice: is your culture work a one-off, or are you building a permanent culture management practice? Organizations at the Managed level in our model choose the latter and are making conscious moves to put into place sufficient people, processes, and support to ensure that their culture design work is not just operational but both continuous and strategic. They are taking their Culture Operations to the next level.

Culture Management Becomes a Thing

At the Managed level the focus on carving time out of people's existing responsibilities (adding headcount starts at Level 4 - Embedded) is less about making room for culture-related projects and more about creating permanent roles and teams to make sure the work gets done. The roles you create will be focused on implementing your culture design work:

Process Owner. For culture management to work, you need a single point of contact, someone who "owns" the process. The role of the process owner is to direct the work of the Culture Teams (see below) and to corral the work of the processes (see below). For very small organizations, this could very well be the CEO. In larger organizations, this role is often assigned to someone from senior management or an individual within Human Resources.

Cross-Functional Culture Teams. Many of our clients created a cross-functional culture team to do the initial culture design work, and as they moved into the Managed level, they made that team a permanent part of the organization, complete with a charter delineating roles, responsibilities, and terms of service. We recommend this team be drawn from multiple departments and multiple layers of the hierarchy; larger organizations may want to create multiple culture teams to focus internally on specific divisions, verticals, or locations.

Local Culture Reps. We frequently see organizations with multiple locations designating local representatives for their culture work (most popular name to date: "Culture Captains"). The people in these roles serve as liaisons between employees at their location and the ongoing work of the Culture Team and focus primarily upon communication.

Processes Enabling Culture Management

Shifting from an ad hoc approach to an intentionally managed approach requires a few new processes, and for culture work that ranges from project management to communications:

Culture Project Management. This may not be the sexy part of culture work, but someone has to manage the implementation of the specific projects that have been designed to move your culture in the right direction, track progress, support accountability, and judge when to bring in new action items (plays in your playbook, as described above) if your current efforts are stalling.

Template for Subgroups. Part of your process should include a template that helps your organization's subgroups (from different locations, verticals, or departments) to design and implement plays specific to their environment.

Culture Metrics. A single culture assessment is a characteristic of the Designed level, but to reach the Managed level, you'll need a more comprehensive metrics strategy for culture that includes measuring the progress and impact of your culture-changing efforts, tracking trends in your employee engagement, and digging into specific elements of employee experience that are relevant to your culture work (around the onboarding process, for example).

Internal Communications. Culture change doesn't work if it's invisible to people, so an internal communications plan is critical. This may involve creating new culture artifacts for sharing or elevating ones you had developed before, but it definitely involves a coordinated effort to ensure that the whole organization is aware of all the moving parts of your new culture management machine.

Support for Culture Management

Culture work must obviously have had organizational support in order to reach the Designed level, but at the Managed level, this support is both broader and deeper in terms of resource commitment and the support of management.

Tactical Culture Budget. Instead of money being pulled from other budgets or reserves to spend on culture work, at the Managed level, the organization commits to an annual culture budget, typically focused on the processes mentioned above.

Senior Leadership. At the Managed level, senior leadership is not only visibly committed to the culture work, it is now more consciously modeling the behaviors of the culture and more frequently in communication with the whole organization regarding cultural concepts and processes. Senior leadership also provides active and visible support to the Culture Team by providing strategic guidance and removing internal obstacles as needed.

Middle Management. To be successful at this level, middle management must buy into culture work, because these managers are crucial to the implementation of plays and other culture management processes. To win them over, make sure they see the value of this work, not only to the organization as a whole but to their own success as middle managers.

Characteristics of a Managed Culture:

- The culture work is supported by solid project management processes.
- You're measuring the progress of your culture work as part of a broader culture metrics strategy.
- An annual culture budget (with a tactical focus) is in place.

There are formal roles, responsibilities, and teams focused on the culture work.

There are solid communications about the culture and ongoing culture work.

- Middle management supports and understands the culture work.

Level 4. Embedded

Moving to Level 4 in the maturity model brings you to the final stage of culture management, where culture becomes woven into the organization's fabric rather than a "thing" that you do periodically. Many of the companies we researched for our books operate at this stage (you'll see some examples below), and we find them to be exceptions rather than the norm, but they serve as excellent role models for organizations that want to reap the benefits of a systematic approach to culture.

When you get to Level 4, you'll take the initial work you did in Level 3—putting into place the right people, processes, and support required for sustainable culture work— and transform it into a mature Culture Operations infrastructure. Instead of adding or changing specific processes or adding new responsibilities to people's jobs, you're actually embedding culture into your operations as a whole, primarily within Human Resources, but also in areas such as external communications, your physical space, and organizational policies.

Embedding Culture into Human Resources

The lion's share of effort for this level will be focused on HR. Nearly every-thing HR does can be done differently if you embed culture into the process, and culture cannot be properly nurtured and developed if core people opera-tions are not aligned with culture... so, HR, get ready to roll up your sleeves.

Recruiting/Hiring. "Hiring for culture fit" becomes a reality at this level, not just a platitude. The core elements of culture become the driving force in decisions about where to recruit and how to evaluate candidates, rather than being add-on questions at the end of an interview.

On-boarding. This overlaps with internal communications from the pre-vious level, but here, embedding culture requires that every new employee understands what your culture is—in a deep way—and how it drives the suc-cess of both the organization and its employees. This means you'll redesign your new employee orientation program to be much more comprehensive than a 20-minute video or 300-page manual.

Performance Management. How you evaluate employees and support them in improving performance must be connected to your organiza-tion's culture. This will impact the method you use for collecting and delivering feedback and may influence your overall compensation strategy as well.

Professional Development. Embedding culture into your professional development and learning strategy requires a more nuanced approach, where the skills and knowledge that are developed must be carefully aligned with the cultural behaviors that drive success.

Culture Operations Staffing. At this level, you'll finally start adding posi-tions, typically within HR, that are 100% devoted to culture work. In addition to the tactical culture budget that was established at Level 3, the new Culture Operations staff will have a budget for managing and implementing deeper embedding efforts.

Embedding Culture into Communications

At the previous level, the focus was on internal communications, but in Level 4 the focus is external. Culture must be embedded into the story you tell to the outside world about who you are and what it's like to work in your company.

Employer Branding. This is technically the communications side of the recruiting/hiring process mentioned above, but it's critical that the promises you make to candidates about your workplace culture align with their experiences once they join the team.

External Communications. Your overall branding and communications should also reflect your culture in meaningful and visible ways. At a minimum, this can include sharing your core values or the "culture code" on your website, but you can also go deeper and start embedding specific language into all communications that reflect who you are and how you operate.

Embedding Culture into Operations

At this level in the maturity model, your Chief Operations Officer will be getting on the culture bandwagon.

Physical Space. Choosing to design your office space and facilities based on the principles and behaviors in your culture (as opposed to what the architects tell you or to maximize efficiency) reflects a seriousness in your approach to culture that we don't frequently see. The challenge here is to make decisions based on the alignment of your culture and your success drivers instead of adopting popular approaches (e.g., open office design).

Policies. There are a host of organizational policies that should be carefully aligned with culture, including dress code, teleworking, parental leave, purchasing authority, etc. These policies were often written up before the organization clarified its culture, but since they are mostly in the background, they sometimes fail to get updated. Level 4 organizations don't let that happen.

Characteristics of an Embedded Culture:

- Culture is baked into your core talent acquisition and retention practices.
- Some of your HR FTEs are 100% focused on culture.
- Your website tells your culture story effectively to the outside world.
- Your policies are updated and aligned with your culture.
- You have redesigned your office space with culture in mind.

Level 5. Integrated

At this, the final stage of our model, culture and leadership essentially become one thing. Our definition of leadership is adapted from one by Peter Senge, a systems-thinking expert and author of the management classic, The Fifth Discipline:

> Leadership is the capacity within an organization to shape
> its future.

Leadership is an organizational capacity—not a position, individual, or even a set of individual skills (though they are related). Organizations that intentionally develop leadership as a capacity throughout the entire organization will be able to shape their future—that is, a future in which they are successful. Culture, when it is continuously aligned with success, is thus a part of leadership. At Level 5 in our model, this perspective comes to life.

This means that key aspects of organizational life traditionally seen as distinct from culture (e.g., strategy, governance) are now fully integrated.

That's what sets Level 5 organizations apart— they understand that the distinction between any organizational discipline and culture is ultimately false and are forging a new leadership path in the way they embrace this new work of culture. There is really no end to the integration work; it is constant and touches every corner of the organization. We can, however, point to some examples of what it looks like, so you can craft a strategy for getting there.

Vision and Growth

An organization's vision, and the growth targets implied, must connect directly to culture. Frankly, if you pursue growth without considering any cultural implications, you've jumped back to Level 0 in this model, where culture evolves by default instead of design. It doesn't matter which vision or growth targets you choose; you just need to integrate culture. We've seen companies funded by private equity that fine-tune their culture specifically to enable rapid growth. But we've also seen companies like Menlo Innovations, a small software company, that accepts limited growth in order to preserve a successful culture. Menlo built its culture around a series of core processes, one of which is the continuous visibility of its clients to the work Menlo employees are doing on their products. This includes clients coming on-site, on a weekly basis to provide input on decisions about what gets done. Exponential growth may end up being fundamentally incompatible with such a culture, partially due to the logistics of scaling that core practice but also due to the inherent difficulty of finding clients who want to work with their developers that way. And Menlo is okay with that.

They always have the option to change their culture to accommodate more growth, but one decision would not be made without the other.

Strategy

For the record, integrating culture and strategy does NOT mean creating a "culture" category in your strategic plan. Culture is not a strategic initiative— culture is something that should be integrated into all your strategic initiatives, which has important implications. We spoke with a large professional service firm whose staff was struggling with a clash between their internal culture and the culture of some of their clients, where their consultants effectively worked full-time. Our response to this challenge caught them a bit off guard:

Maybe you need to choose your clients more carefully.

That was easy for us to say, of course, standing on the sidelines, but when you integrate culture into strategy you'll end up thinking differently about who you take on as clients, what markets to enter, and what products/services to offer. Level 5 cultures don't ignore the cultural implications of these strategic choices.

Governance

Both nonprofit and for-profit organizations are frequently governed by Boards of Directors (and related bodies). While these groups are technically external to the organization and its staff, they are still part of the culture. In fact, if you believe, as we do, that culture is a fundamental driver of organizational success, then culture is inherent in a Board's fiduciary responsibility. That means Boards must understand the culture, figure out how to support an organizational culture that is aligned with success, and even pay attention to their own culture and how it might be getting in the way.

We worked with a scientific society whose Executive Director realized that the governance structure, while very good at engaging a large number of volunteers in the work of the society, had evolved to a point where decision-making had slowed down to roughly one big decision per year. To turn this around, he engaged the volunteers in a culture assessment that revealed the patterns around their lack of agility and set them down a path of governance reform. If you want to take a systems approach, you need to work on all levels of the system.

Networks

The previous two levels involved extensive work in building out your culture operations function, including cross-functional culture teams, full-time HR staff working on culture, and culture budgets, all of which are critical for the practice of culture. Level 5 is more about culture becoming a way of life; in addition to structures and processes, you'll need to infuse culture into the living networks inside your organization. It is through our networks that we navigate organizational life, so when it comes to understanding and living your culture, these networks must contain the right people.

Quality Living Incorporated is a healthcare company that created an internal designation system related to culture. The top tier, called "Mentors," represents only 5% of the company. Mentors come from every layer in the hierarchy and across different departments and are chosen based on how well they themselves live the culture. They get training with the CEO every month on the different elements of the culture as well. Below that they have a slightly larger group called "Professionals", who also have deep knowledge of the culture. They created and nurtured these two networks to ensure that everyone in the organization would have access to real people who could help them live the culture more fully.

Characteristics of an Integrated Culture:
- Culture is infused into strategic planning and decision-making.
- Decisions about organizational growth keep culture in mind.
- Governance bodies are aware of culture and change it when needed.
- There are active internal networks designed to keep culture alive in people's behavior and approach.

Whatever You Do, Do Something

As mentioned at the top of this Appendix, we chose the golden ratio spiral as a graphic representation of our maturity model for a reason. While there exists a linear progression across different stages and levels via that spiral line, the truth remains that all the levels are still contained within that one big rectangle. This means that as you work to develop your maturity in culture management you can expect to be working on several levels at the same time. It also means that you're never too far away from bouncing back down a few levels of maturity if you stop paying attention. The new work of culture is complex.

We recommend that you embrace that complexity and start being more strategic about building your capacity to do the new work of culture. Understand which pieces of which levels in this maturity model you already have in place, and invest your resources either in deepening those areas or in creating the pieces that are missing.

The path forward varies from organization to organization. Some might realize they invested too much effort into building culture into their external communications (Level 3), before really being clear about which elements of their culture were driving their success (Level 2), and should redirect their efforts accordingly. Others might be faced with a high volume of new hires, which would put integrating culture into their hiring process higher on their agenda, ahead of some elements at lower levels in the model. There is not one, single way to do the work of culture. You'll have to find your own path.

But whatever you do—do something! We believe that the days when you could thrive despite your culture being mediocre are coming to an end. If you want your company to be exceptional, set your sights on the higher levels of culture management maturity. You may not get there overnight, but the sooner you start down the path, the farther ahead of your competition you'll be.

Finding Jamie and Maddie on the Interwebs

LinkedIn

https://www.linkedin.com/in/jamienotter
https://www.linkedin.com/in/maddiegrant

Consulting

https://propelnow.co

Speaking

https://jamienotter.com

Blog

https://propelnow.co/learning

Resources for this book

http://culturechangemadeeasybook.com

Printed in the USA
CPSIA information can be obtained
at www.ICGtesting.com
LVHW012120210924
791605LV00004B/13